Chinese Jade of Five Centuries

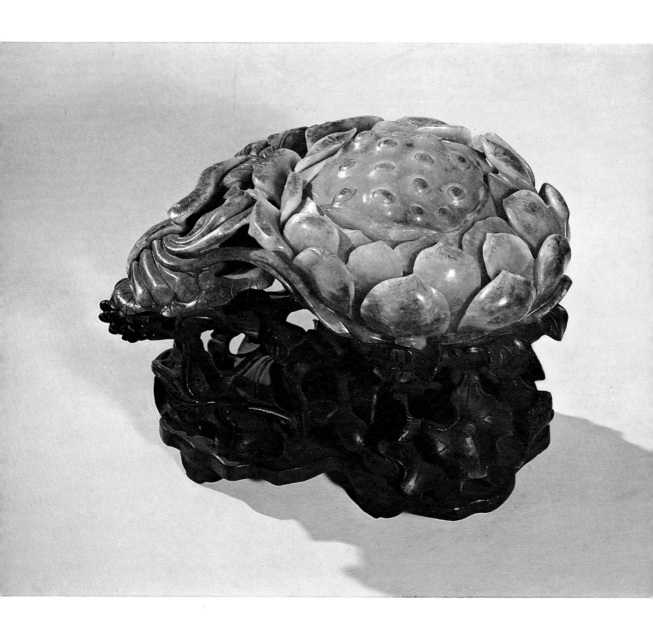

JOAN M. HARTMAN

Chinese Jade

of

Five Centuries

CHARLES E. TUTTLE COMPANY: PUBLISHERS

Rutland · Vermont & Tokyo · Japan

Representatives

Continental Europe: BOXERBOOKS, INC., *Zurich*
British Isles: PRENTICE-HALL INTERNATIONAL, INC., *London*
Australasia: PAUL FLESCH & CO., PTY. LTD., *Melbourne*
Canada: M. G. HURTIG, LTD., *Edmonton*

Published by the Charles E. Tuttle Company, Inc.
of Rutland, Vermont & Tokyo, Japan
with editorial offices at
Suido 1-chome, 2-6, Bunkyo-ku, Tokyo

Copyright in Japan, 1969, by Charles E. Tuttle Co., Inc.
All rights reserved
Library of Congress Catalog Card No. 69-12077
International Standard Book No. 0-8048-0099-5
First printing, 1969

Book design & typography by F. Sakade
Layout of plates by S. Katakura

PRINTED IN JAPAN

To ALAN
without whose encouragement and infinite patience
this book would never have been

Table of Contents

List of Illustrations   *Page* 11

Preface   13

Acknowledgments   17

Periods of Ming and Ch'ing Dynasties   18

Introduction   19

I   The Ming Dynasty *(Plates 4–12)*   37

II The Ch'ing Dynasty   65

    SHUN-CHIH *(Plate 13)*   66

    K'ANG-HSI *(Plates 14–24)*   69

    YUNG-CHENG *(Plates 25–26)*   98

    CH'IEN-LUNG *(Plates 27–45)*   102

    End of the CH'ING DYNASTY *(Plates 46–51)*   146

Conclusion   161

Glossary   163

Bibliography   165

Index   166

List of Illustrations

Asterisks (*) indicate color plates.

*1. (*Frontispiece*) Gray-and-brown nephrite lotus coupe   3
2. Lotus box of gray-green nephrite   28
3. Gray-and-brown nephrite lotus coupe   28
*4. Gray-green nephrite goose   46
5. Gray-green jade vessel in form of owl   48
6. Mountain carving of olive green nephrite   50
7. Buddha's hand citron of gray-green nephrite   52
8. (*Two views*) Sage green nephrite bowl   54
9. Sage green nephrite water buffalo   56
10. (*Two views*) Bowl of oxidized brown jade   58
11. Brown nephrite *pi*   60
12. (*Two views*) Marriage bowl of spinach jade   62
13. Altar chariot vase of white jade   66
*14. Yellow jade vase with dragon and phoenix birds   76
15. White jade dragon group   78
16. Twin-fish group of gray nephrite   80
17. White jade water buffalo with small boy   82
18. Yellow jade libation vessel   84
19. Gray-green jade vessel with dragons   86
20. White jade bronze-form vase   88
21. White nephrite mountain carving   90
22. White nephrite beaker-form vase   92
23. White jade scepter   94
24. Spinach jade double-gourd vase   96
25. White jade water jar   99
26. Yellow jade libation vessel   100
*27. Sage green jade brush holder   108

28. White jade jar with cover   110

29. White jade brush washer   112

30. White jade water pot   114

31. White jade vase   116

32. White jade bronze-form vase   118

*33. Rust brown and white jade vase   120

*34. Brown-and-white jade winged chimera   122

35. White jade libation vessel   124

36. White jade dragon bottle   126

37. White jade bowl   128

38. Moss green jade pilgrim vase   130

39. Spinach jade *hu*   132

40. Bronze-form vessel of dark olive green jade   134

*41. *Fei t'sui* jadeite incense burner   136

42. Covered libation vessel of moss green jade   138

43. Spinach jade pitcher   140

44. Gray-green nephrite bronze-form vessel   142

45. White jade covered vase   144

*46. Green jadeite incense burner   148

47. White jade vase   150

48. *(Two views)* Sage green jade marriage bowl   152

49. Green jadeite Kuan-yin   154

*50. Green jadeite figure group   156

*51. Kuan-yin of lavender jade   158

Preface

There is a tendency to scorn Chinese jade of the 14th through 18th centuries as being inferior, one of the minor decorative arts, not worthy of inclusion in the fine arts category. Scholars are preoccupied with ancient civilizations. There is an aura about broken bits of pottery and corroded bronze tools which sometimes defies comprehension. Granted, these specimens do provide an insight into the culture of people who lived a few thousand years ago and are fascinating from an archeological point of view. But aesthetically speaking, we cannot favorably compare the crude, rough form of a jade *pi* or *ts'ung* to the warm, sensitive figure of the buffalo (Plate 9) from the Ming dynasty or the stately splendor of the white jade covered jar (Plate 28) of the Ch'ien-lung period. It is ludicrous to discuss the beginnings of the medium in the minutest detail, and then proceed to simply discount the fully developed artistic quintessence of the later carvings. Tomb jades have their special place in the first chapters of the story of Chinese art, but for pure artistic accomplishment these later jades cannot be equaled.

Jade carving is an art form. And art is a reflection of the joys, dreams, and fervent beliefs of the people who create it. I have tried to convey the traditional Chinese philosophy and way of life by including brief descriptions of the court, pertinent historical data, and through an interpretation of the symbolism which appears on these jades. This approach is not new, as Couling averred: "A study of the objects made in this hard stone is of inestimable value for the comprehension of Chinese psychology"[8].*

There has certainly been too much unfactual, overly romantic nonsense written on the subject. By the same token, however, it is a pity to discuss this beautiful sculpture in dry, technical terms on the assumption that accuracy is preferable to any attempt at appreciation. So I have endeavored to combine fact with an awareness of aesthetics and the nature of man. In the final analysis it is the Chinese people who shine forth in these jade carvings, their reverence for the stone ascribed to by Confucius when he stated, ". . . wise men have seen in jade all the different virtues. It is soft, smooth and shining, like kindness; it is hard, fine and strong, like intelligence; its edges seem sharp, but do not cut like justice; it hangs down to the ground, like humility; when struck, it gives a clear, ringing sound, like music; the stains in it, which are not hidden and which add to its beauty are like truthfulness; its brightness is like Heaven, while its firm substance, born of the mountains and the waters, is like the Earth. *The Book of Poetry* says, 'When I think of a wise man, he seems like jade.' That is why wise men love jade" [18].

Chinese art has always been of interest to Americans, as witness the great connoisseurs of the turn of the century—J. P. Morgan, Benjamin Altman, Heber R. Bishop, T. B. Walker—and the tradition continues with men like Avery Brundage, whose collection of Oriental art is now housed at the de Young Museum in San Francisco.

The author has traveled throughout the United States

* Numbers in brackets refer to entries in the Bibliography at the back of the book.

in search of jade, and has purposely selected examples from U.S. museums only, as most of these collections have received little attention recently. The pieces herein are but a sampling of the rich treasure in American galleries.

Quite a few of the jade carvings in this volume are not on exhibition at present. It is deplorable how much jade and other fine art is hidden away in museum storerooms! There are, of course, some pieces which are so close in style to that which is already on display that it would be superfluous to exhibit them. I suggest that perhaps these articles could be loaned to other museums whose collections are not as adequately endowed. Again, there are jades which do not meet museum standards of quality. Possibly these pieces could be lent to schools for study purposes. In any case, I hereby make an urgent plea for a clean sweep so that jades and other objets d'art, as well, will once again reflect the light of day and we will all have the opportunity to reap their aesthetic rewards.

JOAN M. HARTMAN

Acknowledgments

Writing a book of this kind necessitates calling upon others for assistance in acquiring pertinent information, photographs, and so forth. My sincere thanks to the following: Mr. Robert Logan, American Museum of Natural History; Mr. Usher Coolidge, Fogg Art Museum; Miss Eleanor Olson, the Newark Museum; Mr. Jack R. Mc-Gregor, Mr. Rene-Yvon D'Argence, and Mr. Clarence Shangraw of the M. H. de Young Memorial Museum; Mr. E. R. Hunter of the Norton Gallery; Mr. George Switzer of the Smithsonian Institution, and Mr. Robert Crowningshield of the Gemological Institute of America. My thanks go to the staff at the Metropolitan Museum of Art, the Cleveland Museum of Art, the Minneapolis Institute of Arts, the Walker Art Center, the University Museum and the Seattle Art Museum for their cooperation. I should also like to express my appreciation to Dr. Chih Meng and Prof. Chu Chai who have given me a fuller understanding of Chinese art and philosophy, and to Peter Swann who advised me to ''push the doors in'' I am deeply grateful.

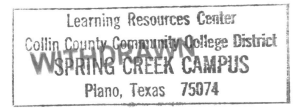
17

PERIODS OF THE MING DYNASTY	Hung Wu	1368–1398
	Chien-wen	1399–1402
	Yung-lo	1403–1424
	Hung-hsi	1425
	Hsuan-te	1426–1435
	Cheng-t'ung	1436–1499
	Ching-t'ai	1450–1457
	T'ien-shun	1457–1464
	Ch'eng-hua	1465–1487
	Hung-chih	1488–1505
	Cheng-te	1506–1521
	Chia-ching	1522–1566
	Lung-ch'ing	1567–1572
	Wan-li	1573–1620
	T'ai-ch'ang	1620
	T'ien-ch'i	1621–1627
	Ch'ung-chen	1628–1644
THE CH'ING DYNASTY	Shun-chih	1644–1661
	K'ang-hsi	1662–1722
	Yung-cheng	1723–1735
	Ch'ien-lung	1735–1795
	Chia-ch'ing	1796–1821
	Tao-kuang	1821–1850
	Hsien-feng	1851–1861
	T'ung-chih	1862–1873
	Kuang-hsu	1874–1908
	Hsuan-t'ung	1909–1912

Introduction

Location of Jade Rough Material

There are distinctly two materials known as jade in the Western world—nephrite and jadeite. The former is found in the mountains and river beds of Eastern Turkestan (near Khotan and Yarkand). It is this nephrite material which was familiar to the ancient Chinese as well as later generations.

Nephrite is also found near Lake Baikal in Siberia. It is uncertain when the Chinese first imported this material, but Hansford suggests that trade began after 1850 [19, pp. 46-48]. As many pieces made of this material are typically 18th century, the question remains open.

Jadeite was originally discovered in the tributaries and valleys of the Uru River near Mogaung, Burma. From the late 19th century on, however, the major source has been the Tawmaw Plateau. While there may have been some jadeite brought to China at an earlier time, there is no conclusive record of this until the latter part of the 18th century, during the reign of Emperor Ch'ien-lung [21, p. 44].

In recent years, small deposits of nephrite and jadeite (the latter reputedly of a similar color quality to Burmese material) have been found on Honshu island, Japan (in Kotaki and Omi); these deposits may have been the original source of material for the numerous jadeite beads excavated from early Japanese Jomon (prehistoric) tombs. There is no evidence, however, that this stone was ever exported to the Chinese mainland. We conclude, then, that the jadeite known to the Chinese was of Burmese origin [36; 52].

The preceding simply clarifies a few points which are sometimes misunderstood, and leads us to perhaps the most astonishing fact of all. Despite varying accounts to the contrary, no definite proof has been established that either nephrite or jadeite was ever quarried in China proper! Some authorities have translated references to jade from Chinese classical writings, but it has been pointed out that the word *yü* or its calligraphic equivalent 玉 also refers to other minerals and sometimes signifies qualities such as beauty, purity, splendor, and the highest honors, rather than a particular stone. *Yü* does not pertain to jadeite. The Chinese call this Burmese stone *fei t'sui* after the kingfisher bird which sports a brilliant green plumage. Thus it can be readily seen that the old texts are often misleading.

Jade has been found in other parts of the world. In the United States it is native to Wyoming and California. Large deposits are also found in western Canada and Taiwan. The Maori people of New Zealand, the Eskimos of Alaska, the Aztecs and Mayans of Central America all carved jade which they found *in situ*. The Chinese, however, who had to open trade routes and keep the importation of jade rough flowing over thousands of miles via water and beast of burden not only recognized the intrinsic beauty of the stone but possessed the artistic genius to develop this medium from its early archaic form to the simple refinement of the Ming dynasty, on through the highly decorative Ch'ing dynasty. Of course, it is characteristic of human nature to seek that which is difficult to acquire, to conquer that which offers the most resistance, to assume the task which poses the greatest challenge. The Chinese obviously set out to prove themselves capable of not only mastering the actual cutting procedures, but of creating magnificent works of art which bear witness to their artistic ingenuity.

Jadeite and
Nephrite: Their
Mineral Properties Before we enter upon the study of the jade carvings themselves, it is well to know a few basic facts about material, workmanship, and dating. Nephrite belongs to the amphibole group of minerals, and jadeite is a member of the pyroxene family. A detailed study of the chemical composition of each can be found in Hansford's book, *Chinese Jade Carving* [21]. For our purposes it is sufficient to quote Hardinge, "The wide colour range of the jade-stones is due to the presence, usually in minute quantities, of various metallic oxides, especially those of iron, chromium and manganese" [23]. The color variations are innumerable. Nephrite ranges in color from pale green to moss to spinach, white, gray-white, mutton fat (yellow-white), deep gray, brown, red (rust brown), to black, yellow and combinations thereof. Siberian nephrite is a medium green color flecked with tiny black spots and is often translucent.

Jadeite is generally of purer or more vivid coloring than nephrite due to the presence of chromium, the same element that gives emeralds their rich green color. Jadeite is snow white, emerald green, lavender, blue, and mixtures of these colors. As mentioned previously, a piece of green-and-white jadeite is often called *fei t'sui*. The brilliance of fine jadeite material can be breathtaking! Some years ago, I visited the California home of the late Admiral Yannopoulos, an avid jade collector. Enclosed in a cabinet stood an emerald green, translucent jade incense burner, approximately 9 inches tall by $7\frac{1}{2}$ inches wide, of almost uniform color consistency. The vessel was free of decoration other than the carved loose-ring handles and dragon finial topping the cover, and it bore a high polish, the extreme simplicity of design permitting full appreciation of the material itself. Such pieces are rare, as pure green jadeite is usually found in small specimens suitable for jewelry, seals, palm pieces, etc.

While numerous texts and catalogues refer to "pink" jade, the description is an erroneous one. In every case where the author has come across examples of this color, both in and out of museum collections, tests have proven the material to be other than jade. Sometimes a jade carving is painted on the inside so that a rosy glow is reflected through the translucent material. More often, however, the "pink" jade carving will turn out to be chalcedony quartz, rose quartz, pink garnet, or thulite. Mr. Robert Crowningshield, Director of the Gemological Institute of America, states that in twenty-five years of examining minerals he has never found a carving, geode, or even the tiniest specimen of "pink" jade. We must conclude then that pink jade is non-existent; all statements to the contrary are either honest mistakes or extravagant fancy.

In addition to the color differences between nephrite and jadeite we should consider the matter of surface quality, which further distinguishes the two materials from one another. Nephrite, when polished, takes on a waxy or soapy appearance. Jadeite gleams with a fine gloss. Hansford describes the "lustre of nephrite [as being] oily rather than vitreous and that of jadeite the reverse" [21]. True, the new nephrite carvings made in Peking today sport a high polish in comparison to the older examples. This is probably due, however, to an improvement in the polishing substances used. Nevertheless, jadeite subjected to the same carving and buffing methods assumes a brighter sheen.

These are the easily visible differences between nephrite and jadeite. What about some of the invisible elements which differentiate the two? Hardness is an important factor. Friedrich Mohs' scale is used to determine the hardness of minerals. Nephrite measures 6.50, while jadeite ranks 6.50 to 7 on this scale of 10. The diamond is the hardest stone ranking at 10. So there is a small difference in the hardness of nephrite and jadeite.

Next let us examine the actual consistency of these

materials. Though a bit softer than jadeite, nephrite is fibrous, rendering it a little tougher than its counterpart and consequently more resistant to the cutting tools. Jadeite has a crystalline composition, that is, its structure is made up of crystals. Mr. Crowningshield tells of having seen a shattered jadeite specimen, from the center of which a single prism had fallen out intact. Thus we can understand why both nephrite and jadeite offer individual problems which challenge the skill and capacity of the craftsman.

How to Verify Genuine Jade   The expert can usually determine whether a carving is nephrite or jadeite or neither. He is aware of color, polish, and mineral composition. But even the experienced are fooled occasionally. There are many stones which imitate jade. Why care if the carving is jade or not as long as it looks as good? Why is a carving more valuable because it is jade rather than serpentine (sometimes called onion jade or new jade), soapstone, green quartz, green garnet, chrysophrase, smithsonite, or chalcedony? The answer is a multiple one. First of all, fine jade rough is available in very limited quantities. Secondly, other minerals which bear a strong resemblance to jade generally do not exhibit the beautiful color properties of nephrite and jadeite. Last but not least, jade is more durable than its imitators. As usual, there is no satisfactory substitute for the real thing.

Minerologists have devised various tests to establish whether or not a particular example is genuine jade. The simplest method is to attempt to scratch the surface of the stone with a sharp blade. Theoretically, if it scratches it is not real jade. However, certain quartzes and types of serpentine are virtually as hard as jade and will not yield to the knife blade or razor edge. Hence the scratch test is not conclusive. Recently, further difficulty has arisen with the advent of stainless steel razor blades. These harder instruments will bite into genuine jade material, so this test is indecisive.

Nephrite has a specific gravity of from 2.90 to 3.20 and jadeite measures 3.20 to 3.50. Small carvings such as snuff bottles can be immersed in a heavy liquid such as bromoform, the density of which will permit the false jade to float, the heavier genuine jade to sink. This method is not recommended for pieces which have painted decoration or are treated (tinted) in any way, as the chemical liquid is likely to remove the color.

Sir Charles Hardinge notes that experiments were done by the Freer Gallery in submitting jadeite and nephrite to extreme heat. At a temperature of 1,025° centigrade, jadeite liquified to a colorless glass and dried to a distorted shape, while nephrite changed to a yellowish, opaque substance resembling calcined bone [23]. The latter case brings to mind certain examples of jade carving which are thought to have changed color due to exposure to fire or extreme heat (Plate 10).

Obviously the collector, considering what may turn out to be the most prized addition to his cabinet, is not desirous of subjecting it to scratches, drowning, burning, and other means of mutilation! The researchers may keep their share of adventure and we are most grateful for their findings, but it is suggested that when in doubt you take the article to the nearest gemological laboratory such as the Gemological Institute of America which has branches in New York City and Los Angeles. There they will place the piece under the surveillance of scientific apparatus such as the spectroscope and the refractometer. These machines measure the optical physical properties of the material against established standards. The piece will be returned in its original condition and the verdict given with assurance.

Chloromelanite There is another stone, officially classified as jade, to which very little reference is made in textbooks, namely, chloromelanite. This is jadeite found in Burma. Due to large amounts of iron in its composition, chloromelanite at its best is a deep, rich green color. It is also found in shades of dark green and black. Somewhat like malachite in appearance, the material lacks translucency and has a heavy, almost synthetic look. It does take on the high polish characteristic of jadeite, but generally speaking carvings of this material are clumsy and ungraceful. In recent years, a good number of chloromelanite carvings have been sold on the open market. Probably because of their brilliant green color the prices have been formidable. Nevertheless, the thick, plastic-like quality of this material does not really satisfy the keen aesthetic taste.

A material similar in appearance to chloromelanite, called *maw-sit-sit* by the Burmese and classified officially as chromealbite feldspar, has been available for the past few years. Its color has a bluer cast than jadeite and the veining varies considerably from the genuine jade. Once again, however, it is advisable to submit the example to reliable testing procedures for absolute certainty.

Japanese
Jadeite
In addition to the small finds of Japanese jadeite mentioned earlier, an inferior material has been carved in Japan recently, its appearance quite different from the Burmese stone. "Japanese jade" has a pale green to white ground spotted with green and black flecks and is not translucent. In contrast to the Burmese material it does not take a high polish. Thus, while being the genuine article it lacks the lovely appearance of its Burmese relative.

"Imperial"
Jade
The term "Imperial" was originally applied to jade carvings which came from one of the imperial palace collections. As such, these examples were of the highest caliber. We often hear pieces described as "Imperial green jade" or "Imperial white jade" and assume that reference is being made to nephrite or jadeite carvings of the finest quality. However, in recent years it has become common practice to label almost any jade carving as "Imperial" for commercial purposes. In fact the term has been bandied about so carelessly that it no longer carries any legitimacy and should be taken with a grain of salt

when heard. One must rely upon one's own knowledge or that of a trusted adviser to determine whether a jade carving is of superlative quality, average, or not worthy of consideration. Name tags mean nothing.

Carving Jade   The actual fashioning of a jade sculpture is a remarkable, arduous procedure. To begin with, a portion of the outer covering or rind of the boulder is cut away and polished to reveal the inner color qualities or veins of the material. It is then decided, according to shape, size, and color composition, the subject best suited to the rough. In modern factories, the manager of the shop makes this decision and draws the design on the jade hulk itself. He then hands the cutting job to the first of many workmen who will contribute his particular talent to the whole. Each carver specializes in one or more phases of the carving process. So a finished carving is the creation of a number of craftsmen who have combined their talents to fashion a work of art. This system did not always exist. It probably came into being during the Ming dynasty and fully blossomed in the period of K'ang-hsi and Ch'ien-lung.

The working of jade is done by hand-operated, simple machinery equipped with tools similar to dentists' drills. Power for the various steel cutting implements is derived from electricity in more modern factories, but up to recent times the gears were turned by a foot-treadle process much like our old fashioned sewing machines. There are many different sizes and shapes of tools employed to execute the splitting of a boulder, the hollowing out of a bowl, the intricate incising of motif, the delicate completion of a loose-ring chain, each requiring the appropriate cutting instrument.

But it takes more than steel to cut jade, for the operation is fundamentally a grinding or wearing away of the stone. Crushed "sand" is used in conjunction with the cutting tools. Hansford has written that up to the time of the collapse of the Manchus in 1912 this sand consisted of quartz, almandine, garnets, and black corundum.

Today the most popular abrasive is a synthetic material known as carborundum. This wet abrasive is spread upon the jade rough by hand and replenished periodically. Slowly, tediously, using these very primitive means, the natural rock is shaped into the finished vase, incense burner, mountain of the most precise detail. The last step, that of polishing the completed article, is accomplished with a buffing wheel and a paste called *pao yao* made of carborundum and other sands found in China.

Undoubtedly, in earlier times there were individual artists who conceived the original design and carved the jade in its entirety. Much to our regret, however, jade carvings were rarely signed by the artist. And to make things more difficult, the names of jade craftsmen have neither been recorded nor are they mentioned in old Chinese literature (see page 30). We do note a definite similarity of design in a great many jade carvings, but often come across a piece which is unique in subject, of unusually fine detail, showing an understanding of the material which goes beyond the everyday encounter. Many of the older carvings, particularly those attributed to the Ming dynasty, have this distinguishing quality; each piece being a work of art in itself, displaying the imaginative ability and inspiration inherent to the Chinese lapidary alone.

Richard Gump speaks of the Chinese jade artist as follows: "Many aspects of his craft were traditional, yet no two pieces of jade were the same; each was in itself a new challenge. His greatest talent lay in his acute sensitivity to the stone. He had to know the stone intricately, aware of every flaw and imperfection, intuitively sensing its concealed virtues and potentialities. He was constantly aware of its limitations, yet knew he could do with this material what could never be done with any other. . . . His eyes had to be able to see below the surface of the stone, judging how far a streak of color would penetrate, in which direction it would turn" [17].

The artist might reach a point in the working of a piece

only to find brown or green or black areas which were not evident before. It was his decision to incorporate the bit of color in the carving of foliage, the face of a figure, the wing tips of a bird, the finial of a cover or simply cut the tone out completely, provided it did not run right through the material. He could take a piece of white jade and create an elaborately decorated vessel such as the one from the Seattle Art Museum (Plate 30) or fashion the same material into a very simple marriage bowl like the one from the Minneapolis Institute of Arts (Plate 37). Nature and man joined forces to produce a unique work of art.

Just as there is a difference in the technique of the bronzes of Degas and Rodin, careful inspection will reveal a marked contrast in "hand" quality from one jade carving to another. For instance, two similar pieces of the Ming dynasty offer quite individual interpretations of the same subject. Plate 2 *(facing page, above)* is a lotus box of gray-green nephrite, $2\frac{1}{4}$ inches tall, in the Eugene Fuller Memorial Collection, Seattle Art Museum. Plate 3 *(below)* is a gray-and-brown nephrite lotus coupe or water receptacle, in the Metropolitan Museum of Art (see also frontispiece). Both pieces are of a like subject and are done in the "heavy" form typical of this era. Both have a soft, dull wax polish. However, one can perceive a difference in cutting technique or dexterity of hand. While each example is a strong representation, Plate 2 exhibits more grace in the flower petals turned slightly under, the almost scroll effect of the stems, the very delicate up-sweep of the veined leaf which manages to enwrap the pod. There is a swaying, nearly rhythmical aspect to the whole, punctuated by the very well-controlled reticulation. In comparison, the coupe in Plate 3 is crudely carved. The flower petals are powerfully shaped but have a stiff, taut appearance. The accent lines on the petals and the leaf at lower left are carelessly, primitively drawn. Though there is a pleasant swirling curve running from the end of the flower into the group of stems, the cutting lacks the delicacy and symmetry apparent in the piece from

Seattle. Thus we can see that while these two sculptures appear virtually the same at first glance, careful scrutiny reveals definite differences in "hand" quality.

Dating Jade   It is my firm belief that the reason comparatively few scholars have chosen to discuss jades of the later periods is not because these carvings lack artistic validity, but because it is exceedingly difficult to date them accurately. As stated before, jade carvings which bear the signature of an artist are the exception rather than the rule. I have found just three references to particular artists in this field. Dr. Cheng Te-k'un mentions Luh Tzu-kang who lived in the late Ming dynasty, describing the artist as a well-respected calligrapher and painter who, "worked only on fine mutton-fat jade and was reputed to have produced exceptionally fine examples which were unrivaled by any others in the art." He then goes on to describe a white jade pendant in his possession which is signed by this artist. Further on, however, Dr. Cheng admits, "It would be difficult to prove that this is actually the work of Luh Tzu-kang himself, but it seems safe to conclude that it was at least carved in his style" [7, p. 34].

Two other carvers are mentioned by Na Chih-liang [38, p. 18]: a 16th-century carver of jade seals known as Wang Shin-lu, and a 17th-century carver, Wang Hao-chen; the latter once stated that after carving jade it was difficult for him to work common stone for it was "as soft as bean curd." The reader will note that these references discuss smaller jade pieces, so that when it comes to the larger, more important examples we are still completely in the dark as to the particular artist or artists responsible for the work.

Eighteenth-century jade carvings usually have a more practiced, professional appearance. Many were produced in factories on an assembly-line basis, with one workman shaping the rough, another incising the design, another cutting the loose-ring chain, another buffing, while all the carvers worked from a master drawing executed by the foreman of the shop. While this system was common practice, there is no lack of variety in jade design. And there were, undoubtedly, individual artists who worked alone, carving the stone from start to finish according to their own inspiration. Which of these jade carvings is the product of one hand rather than several? We do not know.

Occasionally, one finds a carving with the reign mark of the Emperor Ch'ien-lung or another monarch, or a poem by the same illustrious personage, but we cannot guarantee that the object is actually of the period. Reign marks were often added later, sometimes to new pieces, but even more frustrating is the fact that one finds jades which by all present standards appear to be K'ang-hsi (early 18th century) or older, well marked with the Ch'ien-lung reign (late 18th century) underfoot! Of course, the presence of an imperial mark can merely indicate that the jade was part of the emperor's collection, the object actually fashioned at an earlier time. This theory would seem valid when we consider Chinese ceramics (a few from the Ming dynasty and quite a number of the Sung dynasty) which are inscribed as having been part of the imperial collection of Ch'ien-lung.

When a piece of jade is excavated from a Chou dynasty tomb the attribution is a sure one, and we can then compare other items of the same nature to determine dating. But the jades of the 14th to 19th centuries have, for the most part, been handed from one generation to another with little record of ownership or origin. Consequently, there are a great many pieces—too many—which graced the imperial palace in Peking before the Boxer Rebellion. There are no accurate records to substantiate the earliest background of these jades, no signatures to compare, no outmoded or lost skills to cite, few clues to aid us in attributing individual works to specific periods in Chinese history.

While authorities agree that the basic skills for cutting jade were fully developed by the end of the Chou dynasty, they admit that both tools and polishing substances were improved and refined as years went by. Needless to say, with better means at his disposal the lapidary was able to achieve new heights in artistic accomplishment.

In tracing jade carvings from the Ming through Ch'ing dynasty, we see a very definite transition in style and workmanship. Ming jades, as illustrated in this book, display a simplicity of form, rounded elementary lines, a heavy hand and almost no polish, or a soft-paste surface. The material is usually a dull nephrite—gray, black, spinach green, brown, pale celadon, white—frequently with burnished gold or rust highlights; materials in colors not often seen in later periods. The reason for the use of comparatively dull or somber material lies in the fact that jade rough was rather scarce at this time. The Chinese were not on friendly terms with their Western neighbors and this circumstance must have cut jade traffic considerably. Hence, the carving of whatever material was available, despite its dreary color.

Another characteristic of Ming jades is that their subjects are traditional. Confucius meditates with his disciples against a forest background. Libation vessels and other altar pieces bearing resemblance to the ancient bronze-forms are prevalent. Under whose imperial reign in the Ming dynasty (A.D. 1368–1644) was a particular example made? We can only conclude that the more primitive pieces are of an earlier time; the precise, well-worked compositions of a later date.

Jade carvings of the Ch'ing dynasty (A.D. 1644–1912) are generally more elaborate than the earlier pieces. From the K'ang-hsi period on, the traditional designs were embellished and a freedom of expression was granted the artist. It was no longer necessary to adhere strictly to the old forms. One finds vases with dragons climbing aloft, intricately executed lotus-form coupes, animals with pronounced detail. The carving begins to show accuracy and dexterity and unrestrained motif. The typical K'ang-hsi specimen is carved of a pale celadon-white nephrite with touches of brown on the surface (Plate 17). However, we do find carvings in fine white nephrite, spinach, mutton fat, and yellow material, too. The polish, however, remains soft and waxy like that of the Ming pieces. Hence, those carvings which break away from the traditional subject matter, but boast the same velvety surface quality as that of the older pieces, can usually be associated with the K'ang-hsi period.

It is virtually impossible to determine whether jades are of the K'ang-hsi or later Yung-cheng (1723–35) period. The latter reign was a short one, and the art very similar to that of the K'ang-hsi era. Corroborating this statement Nott wrote, "Many indeed of the works accredited to this period belong in reality to that of Yung-cheng" [41]. Consequently, we have no choice but to go on to the great Ch'ien-lung period where the style and craftsmanship show a marked distinction from the earlier works.

Jades of this period are even more elaborate than the K'ang-hsi carvings. Just as we find Ch'ien-lung porcelains to be fanciful and ornately decorated, so the jades are enveloped in flowers, birds, and dragons, covered with mythological symbols and religious representations, embellished with long loose-ring chains; sometimes gaudy, yet done with remarkable deftness of hand. There was a pride in innovation, a search for the epitome in design. The material is pure white nephrite, mutton fat, spinach, moss, celadon green and the polish assumes a high sheen. Ch'ien-lung jades are imaginative, lavish, gay, full of a sense of carefree abandon and well being which accurately reflects court life at that time.

As mentioned before, all reliable records indicate that jadeite was not introduced into China, in quantity, until the end of the 18th century—the latter part of Emperor Ch'ien-lung's reign. The brilliantly colored stone became popular overnight. We know, however, that the first objects carved were small hair ornaments, pendants, jewelry, etc. Gump writes, "Chinese jade experts agree that during the last years of the reign of Emperor Ch'ien-lung and for many years thereafter fine jadeite was used almost exclusively for jewelry'' [17]. The large carvings came later, so that comparatively few major works in jadeite actually emanate from the Ch'ien-lung period. Too many jadeite carvings are attributed to this reign. Undoubtedly, many of these pieces are of the Chia-ch'ing, Tao-kuang, and subsequent periods.

We have little information to go on in determining the pieces which belong to the 19th century and later. However, we do note that after the Ch'ien-lung period, jade carving becomes, for the most part, less tasteful. Designs lack finesse, sincerity, artistic integrity. A commercial aspect pervades the medium. The finish is glossy, almost garish in its brilliance and the small, inner areas are often not polished at all, showing a carelessness of execution. Incense burners and tall vases take on a mass-produced, manufactured precision, a rococo air rather than the warmth and purity of the earlier examples. In an introduction to the jade collection of Vassar College, Alfred Salmony wrote that, ''Forced to justify his attributions, he would describe color, surface, shape, ornament and workmanship, the presumption being that evenness of color, soberness of decoration, and perfection of technique plead for a relatively early origin'' [48].

One can write reams of pages on dating jade. There comes a time, though, when words are superfluous. For art is a personal, highly emotional quantity. Pick up a piece of jade. Observe its detail. Feel its surface quality. Examine the material under a light. Put it down and come back to it another day. Continue to examine and handle other jade carvings. Notice the subtle differences in material, carving, polish, subject matter. The appreciation grows upon you. It is only by handling jade over and over again that one acquires an instinctive knowledge of the art, an awareness of style and form and finish which enables one to place the item within a certain period of Chinese history. There are no rigid rules to follow. We can only view the contrasts in workmanship very broadly, and make a carefully considered, calculated guess.

Being unable to identify the artist is a great loss to the serious student of jade art. Think of the keen insight and understandings we have acquired about the paintings of Rembrandt through a knowledge of his life story. How could we fully appreciate the flamboyant colors and subjects of Ruben's murals if we were not acquainted with this dashing aristocrat who felt at home in all the capitals of Europe? Would the pencil drawings and the dabbed paints of van Gogh be quite as moving if we knew nothing of his heartbreaking existence? Alas, we have no choice but to surmise what influences and motivating factors inspired the Chinese jade carver to make of this cold, hard stone a warm responsive work of art full of inferences, suggestions, and clues to the emotional substance of his life.

Yet man will not be daunted. We increase our understanding of jade by considering the function of the object and the symbolism of motif be it religious, mythological, simply decorative, or a blend of the three. With these few guides, and a general comprehension of the events and systems under each imperial reign, we painstakingly put our story together.

The Ming Dynasty

Una Pope-Hennessy once wrote that, "During the clois-
tered period of Ming, China stereotyped herself into the
image we all carry in our minds" [45]. That image is
usually composed of a stately mandarin figure seated upon
an elaborately carved, gilded throne, clad in embroidered
silk, his whiskered face wearing a cold, remote expression
—in brief, the very epitome of dark intrigue and mysticism! Add a swarm of pale, pathetic little women with
tightly bound feet, or the delicate ladies who graced the
imperial court, a smoker's cave reeking with opium, girl
babies abandoned to die, a blue-and-white porcelain vase,
a green jade incense burner, a huge brass gong courtesy
"Movie Moguls, Inc." and you have the popular concep-
tion of Cathay during the Ming dynasty. Though each of
these elements existed, they are but the frosting, the fur
trim, the surface qualities, which no more indicate the
true character of Ming China than Hollywood movies, hot
dogs, the watusi, and Mississippi provide an accurate picture of the United States of America.

The Ming dynasty was founded in 1368 and lasted 276
years. Emperor Hung-wu came to power in triumph, for
he had succeeded in driving the hated Mongol conquerors
back to their nomadic life in the north. The great khans
were through dominating the Chinese people. A Chinese

emperor would provide protection for and administrate over his own countrymen. Apropos of the climate of the time, Rev. J. Macgowan related the story of a magnificent tower which the Mongols had built in Peking. Upon seeing this edifice, Emperor Hung-wu said, "If the Mongols had paid as much attention to the comfort and happiness of their people as they did to building such costly but unnecessary structures as this they would still be the rulers of China today" [32]. He then gave orders to have it completely destroyed "so that not a single trace of it would be left by which posterity could distinguish it." China was for the Chinese. They needed no one but themselves. They were to be self-sufficient, economically and culturally.

It was a big country. Macgowan remarked that the 18 provinces and its colonies measured 1,297,999 square miles. He estimated the population to have been 66½ million in 1412 [32]. Hucker states that the population probably went up to 100 million by the 17th century. In the early years, the army included "more than fifteen thousand officers and more than one million, one hundred thousand soldiers" [25]. It was an agricultural country, composed of small and large villages as well as cosmopolitan cities. Each hamlet, each town lived virtually isolated from the capital, governing itself under the direction of its local leaders who represented imperial rule.

Emperor Hung-wu ascended the throne in what was then the capital city of Nanking. He immediately set about the task of inaugurating reforms and legislation which would serve as guide lines for the nation, and re-establish the purely Chinese culture. Expenditures of the royal household were cut considerably, and strict orders were issued to the effect that money was to be spent prudently and with an eye toward public welfare. To this particular purpose, he even reduced the number of women connected with the royal court. In an effort to encourage education and the arts, the emperor took a personal interest in the Hanlin Academy, offering special prizes and honors for those scholars who passed the examinations and were elected members.

There was a Directorate of Astronomy, a Directorate of Parks, an Imperial Academy of Medicine, a National University, a Supreme Tribunal for criminal cases, and an Office of Transmission which served as a message center to transmit news back and forth from the capital to the smaller provinces. The emperor received periodic reports from his representatives in various areas of the country, who were, for the most part, men born and brought up in the towns they resided in, rather than outsiders the emperor might have placed there. In addition, Emperor Hung-wu regulated taxation and introduced a national currency. Hucker writes, "It was probably the most elaborate and sophisticated governmental system existing in the world in its time" [25]. These early years of the Ming dynasty were blessed with peace and prosperity. In such an atmosphere the creative arts flourished.

The city of Peking became the official capital in 1421. Emperor Yung-lo ordered 100 thousand of the most prosperous, cultured people in the land to pack up their belongings and move with their families to Peking. This was to be a society of the literati!

In planning the "Forbidden City," Grousset remarks that the "aesthetic aspect had to harmonize with very strict astronomical and geomantic considerations" [16, p. 290]. For instance, the four palace buildings were adorned as follows: the Eastern Palace with a blue dragon, the Southern Palace with a red bird, the Western Palace with a white tiger, and the Northern Palace with a dark tortoise. According to Williams these are the Azure Dragon facing east which looks upon the morning sun and is, therefore, symbolic of spring; the Vermilion Bird (Phoenix) facing south and the noon sun which stands for summer; the White Tiger facing west which symbolizes autumn; and the Black Warrior (Tortoise) which faces north and symbolizes winter [56, p. 363]. These four supernatural animals exerted strong influence on national life.

Into the newly built sumptuous complex of buildings surrounded by gardens and waterways known as the Forbidden City moved the emperor and his court. Here was a private world of luxury, supplied with the finest appointments of the day. Porcelain dishes and other table articles were made especially for the use of the imperial household. By the same token, decorative objects and articles used for sacrificial rites were made by imperial command —the best obtainable, often ordered by the emperor himself! Ornately carved furniture filled the huge halls, complemented by porcelain, jade, lacquer ware, scroll paintings. Everywhere was color and warmth and a zest for life.

This enthusiasm and verve is still evident when one looks at the chipped remains of red paint embellished with boldly carved and gilded dragons which decorate the exterior of the imperial buildings. Blues and yellows and greens run rampant in endless profusion atop majestic pagoda roofs, framing doors, outlining windows, cascading down a banister, floating over a bridge. And yet, as we have seen, this potpourri of splendor, which appears to have erupted en masse without master plan, was actually part of a scheme adhering to ancient beliefs in the heavens; the various elements; the creatures of nature which signify prosperity, immortality, abundant crops, numerous progeny, peace—in harmony with the cosmic order.

Hucker mentions that, "The Chinese emperor was considered to be the earthly legate of Heaven . . . he was in turn responsible to Heaven for the goodness and well-being of mankind. Unusual astronomical phenomena were thought to be warnings from Heaven, and emperors were expected to respond to them with ritual acts. Natural calamities, floods, droughts, plagues of locusts, and so on were manifestations of Heaven's active displeasure" [25]. In simpler terms, from ancient times, the emperor was the liaison between heaven and earth. He communicated with the gods on behalf of his people. There were, therefore, innumerable ceremonies for various occasions, and the rituals were performed with the use of appropriate implements and containers made of jade and bronze. In later periods, a great many adaptations of archaic bronzes were made of jade (Plate 42). Whether carved for practical use in religious observance or simply to satisfy the artistic taste, or both, Chinese craftsmen managed to preserve as well as improve upon old designs (Plates 5 and 11).

Although jade was carved in China throughout its history, it is not until the 14th century that we find large numbers of pieces wrought in the round of sizable boulders—ten inches and over. Of course, we have large jade slabs or burial tablets decorated with pictographic symbols and examples of the *ts'ung* from earlier periods, but these are certainly not common. It appears likely then that the skills required to handle the heavier rough and fashion the bulky hard stone into realistic, intricately cut works of art were not widespread until this later date.

Despite the influence of Taoism and the infiltration of Buddhism, Confucianism remained the dominant philosophy of classical China. The emperor even observed its principles while embracing the Buddhist or Taoist faith at the same time. Confucianism was based upon human relationships. Family ties came first. After that, loyalty to the emperor. Hucker writes that, ''Violations of filial piety or other breaches of traditional morality, were punishable by the state. In the very last analysis, government operated in the interests, not of the ruler, but of the Confucian system'' [25]. Thus we cannot overemphasize the importance of Confucianism as a moral standard during the Ming rule, which is clearly reflected in jade carvings of the time (Plate 6).

Buddhism was brought to China from India during the Han dynasty (*circa* A.D. 200). The Chinese loved the color, mysticism and romance of the religion, the belief in the next world and the divine goodness of Buddha. They, nevertheless, adapted the faith to suit their own tastes, embracing the Mahayana or ''Larger Vehicle'' for the most part, rather than the more rigid, exceedingly sober Hinayana doctrine.

Chinese Buddhist art is solemn but grand, stately yet joyful. We have only to look at the wondrous stone sculpture from Lung-men and the vivid paintings at Tun-huang to appreciate the transition from the early Buddhist art of India to the fully developed Chinese interpretation. In the words of Dr. Chih Meng, "Buddhism was Chinaized!"

Emperor Ching-t'ai (1450–57) was a devout Buddhist who built the Temple of Great Happiness in which he and his empress worshiped. At a later date, the Emperor Cheng-te (1506–21) went so far as to declare himself to be a living Buddha. Just as Buddhist influence is seen in other forms of Chinese art, so it prevails in jade sculpture, too (Plate 7).

As indicated before, Taoism was a popular creed, reflected over and over again in the art of the time (Plate 4). Emperor Chia-ching (1522–66) was an ardent Taoist, attracted to the faith chiefly because of its guarantee of immortality. He went so far as to have all the Buddhist temples in Peking torn down. We might assume, then, that due to his vehement beliefs Taoist art motifs were welcomed and Buddhist subjects frowned upon. This intolerant attitude, however, is not typical of the Chinese. Hobson wrote that it was common to "find Buddhism and Taoism living harmoniously together beside the State philosophy of Confucius and even extraneous creeds such as Mohammedanism" [24]. Chia-ching did realize his shortsightedness eventually and in 1566, when his death was imminent, he renounced the faith and ordered all the Taoist altars in the palace destroyed. Yet for over thirty years, Taoism had been the dominant religion of the imperial government. Under the circumstances, it would be easy to conclude again that little if any jade was carved with decoration not expressing Taoist doctrine. This is untrue.

Although the emperor employed the finest workmen to produce jades for his household, there were undoubtedly many craftsmen who supplied jade carvings to local officials and literati whose religious views did not necessarily coincide with those of the emperor. It is also important to remember that China was a very large country, and that the emperor's hand could not rigidly control the religious beliefs of the entire population. Local communities retained their own way of life, and the traditional Chinese town was likely to have a Confucian temple, one or more Buddhist temples, and a Taoist temple, too. The three faiths were often intermingled, as the Chinese have habitually taken the best from each philosophy and according to Dr. Meng "mixed their own religious cocktail!" The Jesuit priest, Matteo Ricci, was appalled at the lack of adherence to *one* supreme faith and he looked upon the religious views of the Chinese as being a terrible hodgepodge of heathen ideas. Referring to the religious art of the country during the reign of Emperor Wan-li (1573–1620) he wrote, "In public squares, in villages, on boats, and through the public buildings this common abomination is the first thing to strike the attention of the spectator" [47]. These "abominations" are, no doubt, considered fine works of art today, and give us an inkling of the sobriety and deep spirit which dominated the atmosphere of the age.

So the Chinese combined the tenets of Confucianism, Taoism, and Buddhism to suit their own needs, adding a dash of pure Chinese folklore to give spice to the brew. Along with the numerous rituals observed for various purposes during the year, they followed a strict moral code. This was a "familistic society." It was common practice to have several generations of one family living in the same household. Due authority and respect were awarded the aged. The eldest male in the family managed all business and financial matters with the assistance of the other male members of the clan. The eldest woman in the family supervised the domestic affairs of the home, with the help of the other women in the house. In this way, illness and strife as well as the happier occasions such as birthdays, marriages, etc., were dealt with by the entire clan. The family was a self-sufficient, working unit and everyone in the group was provided for throughout his life.

On a broader scale, the wealthiest family in the town saw to it that schooling was available to all the people, including those who could not afford to pay for it. Of course, there were villages and poor farm areas where formal education was not obtainable, but when possible the Chinese did not shirk responsibility to their own and those less fortunate than themselves. The state issued its own proclamation of a citizen's duty to his community, based upon Confucian standards and the "familyism" discussed above. Verifying this, Hucker writes that "The community agreement . . . included an exhortation to all citizens . . . to be filial and obedient to their parents, to be respectful to their superiors, to be harmonious within the community, to educate their sons and brothers, to be content each in his lot, and not to do evil" [25].

A great deal of this philosophy remains today, at least among the Chinese living abroad. Communism, for the time being at any rate, has set up its own scheme for existence, although most knowledgeable Chinese feel that this is a transitional or comparatively temporary system which will be modified as conditions improve on the mainland of China. In the United States, Americans of Chinese descent continue to observe the old rules of behavior to a large extent. Hard work is an accepted fact of life. Honesty is understood. Education is essential. Parents are respected by their offspring without question. Friendship is slowly savored and steadfastly held. Divorce is unheard of, and the family takes care of its own. As a result, tabloid sheets rarely, if ever, report a crime having been committed by a Chinese-American citizen. The age-old standards are as applicable today as they were over six hundred years ago!

At its peak of strength and popularity, the Ming dynasty was an enlightened, satisfying, pulsating society, with emphasis on the development of fine arts. Corroborating this view, Peter Swann writes that, "It was the great age of the collector and connoisseur. The Chinese aesthetic became fixed" [51].

As with all good things, this period of contentment came to an end. Though the initial struggle to defeat the Mongols was followed by strong leadership and strict adherence to principle, as time went on the emperors became satiated with riches, power, and lack of purpose. Earnestness of ideals was no longer vitally important. Much of the management and attention to governmental affairs was left to the discretion of the eunuchs who changed policies to suit their own ambitions. Thus by the middle of the 16th century the empire showed signs of growing debilitation. The state repeatedly took action which disregarded the plight of the people it supposedly served. And, of course, enemies invariably choose a time when the opponent is most vulnerable to launch an attack.

The Manchus invaded from the north several different times to plunder and retreat. The Japanese raided the countryside near Shanghai periodically, and in 1593 invaded Korea going on into Chinese territory. The emperor dispatched troops, but the war lasted seven years. And all the while Nurhachi, leader of the Manchus, continued to cross the boundaries in the north, becoming bolder as Chinese resistance weakened. The last Ming emperor, Ch'ung-chen (1628–44), seeing defeat at his doorstep, climbed a hill and hanged himself by his girdle. Of this collapse Macgowan wrote, the Ming dynasty "fell as other dynasties did before it, because of the inherent want of moral qualities, without which no power will ever be tolerated by a people like the Chinese, who demand so high an ideal in their sovereign" [32]. One wonders if in the present situation, history will be inclined to repeat itself; but we are here concerned with art, which has managed to survive many a political upheaval.

Plate 4   Pictured is a 17th-century carving of a goose roosting on the water which appears to flow along beneath it, little wavelets lapping up at its feathers. The carving measures $7\frac{1}{2}$ inches long, $5\frac{3}{4}$ inches tall, and is cut of a gray-green nephrite with vivid yellow-rust highlights. This piece and the lotus coupe (Plate 3) discussed earlier, exemplify the very interesting color properties which Ming jade material often presents, pointing up the fact that these gray dense colors can be just as exciting as the much lauded brilliant greens of a later date.

In Chinese mythology, the goose is believed to be emblematic of marriage, as this species always flies in pairs. It is also assumed that the goose never mates a second time, and since remarriage of a widow was frowned upon by the Chinese, the omen was very much in favor. The lotus flower which enriches the design of the carving, is symbolic of numerous progeny and a contented marital relationship. It is also one of the sacred flowers of Buddhism. Here is one of the puzzles which constantly confront us in studying jade sculpture. Was this carving intended as a wedding gift for a bride and groom? Is the Buddhist influence incidental? Is there a hint of Taoist lore in the use of the lotus and the very sweet portrayal of the bird? Or is this merely a carving of one of nature's creatures in its own habitat? The interpretation is yours to decide. But regardless of the ideographic meaning, here is a tender representation typical of the Ming style.

Walker Art Center, Minneapolis.

Plate 5　This very interesting vessel in the form of an owl is carved of pale gray-green jade and measures 6⅜ inches tall. The bird stands alert, his eyes wide open and wary, obviously waiting to sight his next prey. Typical of the early Ming design, the piece is simply cut and has a soft, waxy surface. It is a stylized adaptation of a bronze form, the owl being a favorite subject in Chou bronzes (1027–256 B.C.) and may have had a cover at one time. Surprisingly enough, the outlines of the creature's physical characteristics are quite modern in execution. For instance, the wing feathers are smoothly swept back in an almost rhythmic manner, the tail feathers are carefully curled, the feet are rounded, the eyebrow is curved, the wormlike pattern beneath the eye is fluid enough to designate, body, flesh, and bulk so that the whole gives one the impression of solidity—a being to be dealt with cautiously.

The Chinese look upon the owl as an ominous creature, the bearer of black tidings, often death. It is conceivable that the bronzes of this subject were used in ceremonies designed to ward off an early demise. In any case, while the bronze image is clearly emuated here, some of the original dryness is gone and in its place we see a spontaneity which hints at the innovations to come.

Seattle Art Museum: Eugene Fuller Memorial Collection.

Plate 6   Here is a jade mountain carving which exemplifies the early Ming mood—an emphasis on the simple life, together with a love of nature and the inner spirit of man: moral principles pondered in quiet meditation. Confucius is seated upon rockery, his horse nearby, a single tree overhead. This massive boulder, 11 inches tall, $16\frac{3}{4}$ inches long, $6\frac{7}{8}$ inches deep, carved with emphatic strokes, of an olive green nephrite with brown areas, speaks well of the dignity and wisdom of the great sage. Its soft polish imparts a peaceful aspect to the whole, and its impressive size indicates the importance of the subject. Confucius said, "In private life, show self-respect; in the management of affairs, be attentive and thorough; in your dealings with others, be honest and conscientious. Never abandon these principles, even among savages" [11].

The esteemed teacher set high standards. It is, therefore, quite fitting that on the reverse of this unusually fine example is an inscription, neatly cut in Chinese script, dedicated to the ancestor of a particular family that owned the mountain at one time. Dr. Nott translated the inscription which is dated, "In the Tenth Year of Chia Ching (A.D. 1805)" and the final line of this tribute to a loved one reads, "The likeness of his qualities were so envisioned in the Jade Boulder that it seemed as though it were a monument to his virtue and benevolence." Nott further explained, "So impressed were the previous owners of the object, with the epitaph which its subject matter held of the Great Sage, that they were impelled to inscribe on the back of the work their own revered ancestor, who incidently was a disciple of Confucius" [41, p. 123].

Norton Gallery of Art: Stanley Charles Nott Collection.

Plate 7   A very beautiful example of Ming jade is this Buddha's hand citron. The fruit, which measures 8 inches long, 5 inches wide, 2½ inches tall, is carved in the form of a coupe, the material a pale gray-green nephrite with touches of reddish brown. Again, we note the simplicity of the shape. Although the stem parts and leaves are well defined, there do not seem to be any extra curlicues or folds unnecessary to the realistic portrayal of the subject. The long, delicately modeled tendrils bend gracefully at the tips giving a gentle, soft impression. Actually, the citron is known to the Chinese as Fo Shou (Buddha's hand) as the tips of the fruit resemble Buddha's hand in the classic position, the index and little fingers pointing up. Here is one of those jades which imparts a spiritual quality and a warmth, emerging to our surprise, from the hard, cold stone.

M. H. de Young Memorial Museum: Avery Brundage Collection.

Plate 8
(Two views)

From the Vetlesen Collection is a heavy, dark sage green bowl possibly intended for use as a wine container. The decoration is strongly cut in the form of dragons working amidst clouds. The bottom of the bowl has a multitude of full, swirling waves. Nott described this motif as follows: "the Dragon god of the Sky pours out his blessings on the parched earth through the medium of the clouds, as evidenced by the water and its waves" [39]. Hansford further verifies the meaning by stating that the dragon was worshiped by the Chinese from early times, as the provider of "abundant rains and successful crops" [22]. But the clearest and possibly the most valid interpretation offered is by Okakura when he describes the dragon as unfolding "himself in the storm clouds," washing "his mane in the seething whirlpools" as he awakens to the activity of the changing seasons [56, p. 131]. The bowl measures 8 inches in diameter and is masterfully executed.

Smithsonian Institution: Maude Monell Vetlesen Collection.

Plate 9   This water buffalo of dark sage green nephrite is, according to Dr.
Nott, an "impressively poised portrayal . . . of more than usual
interest, being typical in its style of design to that of its period's
finest productions" [41, p. 151]. Dated as mid-Ming (*circa* 1500)
the piece measures 11⅜ inches long, 6⅜ inches deep, 4⅝ inches tall.
Being the main farm animal of China, the buffalo has always been
revered and valued by the people. Early Chinese are thought to have
considered this animal to be their river god, presiding over the
waters to guard against evil spirits. Due to its use as a farm animal,
it is also emblematic of spring and agriculture, and is admired for
its everlasting patience and physical strength. These qualities are
clearly depicted here, in the heavy hulk of the animal's body; the
flat, sturdy set of its legs; the long, curved sweep of its tail; the hard,
ridged curves of its horns. The nose is blunt, the eyes large and
vacant, the small ears piquantly pointed, the mouth almost smiling.
This is an accurate depiction, showing the creature as a dull-witted
but powerfully built animal, entitled to man's indulgence, kindness
and respect, for which man will in turn receive loyalty, protection,
and long hours of labor. The composition is simple, the polish a soft
sheen, the over-all effect one of peaceful tranquillity.

Norton Gallery of Art: Stanley Charles Nott Collection.

Plate 10
(Two views)   One of the most appealing, yet curious, pieces of jade the writer has come across is this bowl, measuring $9\frac{1}{2}$ inches in diameter, which was burnt to a deep brownish color sometime in the past. The material is not to be confused with calcified or "chicken bone" jade which has assumed a pale gray-white opaque appearance due to exposure to the earth's components during long years of burial. The bowl is striking because, though its color has been altered, the carving remains clearly discernible. On the exterior and interior of the piece we find intricate networks of melon plants, lavishly interpreted with a gay flare for style. Like the gourd, the melon is considered a symbol of fertility and many children, because of its over-abundant supply of seeds. It is also emblematic of great wealth and success. Whether the bowl was burnt while being used for some form of religious ceremony or suffered the effects of a larger holocaust we cannot determine. It is, nevertheless, a fine example from the mid-Ming period.

Walker Art Center, Minneapolis.

Plate **11**   Ancestor worship goes far back in the annals of Chinese history. By the same token, the Chinese often regarded old or antique subjects as worthy of emulation. It was necessary to completely master the fine art of the past before attempting innovation. Therefore, throughout our study of Chinese jade we find the old forms and decorations repeated.

A magnificent example in point is the very powerful jade *pi* pictured here. This elaborate, weighty piece, measuring $12\frac{1}{4}$ inches long, $8\frac{3}{8}$ inches tall, is cut from a warm brown nephrite material which blends to a soft gray-white, and virtually explodes with energy. Depicted in deep relief and stretching out to right and left in reticulated eaves, are innumerable *k'uei* dragons, their bodies writhing, twisting, and turning in a rhythmic, frenzied motion which serves to enliven the quiet tones of the material itself. The central round doughnut shape is, of course, a copy of the ancient *pi* used in the ritual worship of Heaven, examples of which have been excavated from Shang sites (1523–1028 B.C.). The dragons are in profile as well as fully flat, their faces wild, undeniably ferocious, typical of creatures seen on early bronzes, but here somehow imbued with a special vitality and verve not shared by their antecedents.

American Museum of Natural History: William Boyce Thompson Collection.

Plate 12
(Two views)

The final example of this era is a marriage bowl which measures 15 inches across the handles and is exquisitely carved. The bowl is cut of a dark spinach jade and has no polish (the photo belies this fact). Articulately carved on the interior is a well-balanced bouquet of peony blossoms amidst curling, scrolled leaves. This flower signifies happiness, riches, love, and affection. It is also the sign of spring, the season of the year when crops grow and new life begins. The bat handles which are plainly depicted here represent happiness and longevity. On the exterior of the piece are the Pa Chi Hsiang (Eight Buddhist Emblems of good augury). Hansford describes this group as consisting of the "wheel of law, the conch shell (used as a trumpet in Buddhist worship), the umbrella, the canopy, the lotus, the jar (used as reliquary for the ashes of Buddhist monks), a pair of fish, and the mystic endless knot" [22]. Without going deeply into the significance of each symbol, it can be safely stated that in general the Pa Chi Hsiang represent power, rank, and success throughout life. So we have a marriage bowl decorated with the omens of happiness, love, longevity, and fulfillment of enterprise. The "hand" quality of the cutting is deft, but one can still denote a certain crudeness that marks the bowl as being of the late Ming era. We do see a tendency toward more lavish design, however, a prelude to the coming style of the Ch'ing dynasty.

Smithsonian Institution: Maude Monell Vetlesen Collection.

CHINESE JADE 62

The Ch'ing Dynasty

At the time of the Manchu conquest, the Chinese empire included not only the eighteen provinces (China proper) but Manchuria, Mongolia, Chinese Turkestan, Tibet, and Korea with control over Burma and Annam—a total area of over five million square miles. The population was well over 100 million people. And once again there were foreigners presiding over this mighty land.

Coming from Manchuria, the new rulers were accustomed to a rugged outdoor existence where hunting with bow and arrow, astride swift horses, was the established way of life. They spoke a polysyllabic, alphabetical language in contrast to Chinese which is monosyllabic and non-alphabetical. Nevertheless, they had looked upon the Chinese with much respect for many years, admiring their system of government and schools; even giving their own leader the title of emperor. This healthy regard for Chinese tradition led them to adopt a fairly lenient policy when they finally conquered Cathay, for the Manchus understood that to severely oppress the Chinese would result in destroying the social system and stifling the artistic creativity which they esteemed so highly. They, therefore, sought to incorporate themselves into the culture of the country, by improving the old systems and encouraging the arts, thereby proving their good intentions to the people.

SHUN-CHIH   The first emperor of the Ch'ing dynasty was Shun-chih (1644–61), who spent most of his time on the throne subduing the last vestiges of resistance to the new government. He did manage, however, to revise the system of public examinations for scholars, which had become quite corrupt toward the end of the Ming rule. Those first years were ones of turmoil, and the arts suffered in the confusion of petty politics and undecided loyalties. Very little fine art emanates from this period, but we show one example attributed to the Shun-chih reign, which is well worth a long look.

An elegant "altar chariot vase" (Plate 13) in the Stanley Charles Nott Collection, Norton Gallery of Art, is carved of white jade with a faint green cast [41, p. 175]. Measuring $8\frac{3}{8}$ inches tall, $5\frac{1}{2}$ inches wide, the vase depicts a pair of *fêng huang* birds, their bodies swirled into one, the wing formation somewhat reminiscent of the owl (Plate 5) discussed earlier. The *fêng huang* (phoenix bird) is considered the most magnificent and respected of all feathered creatures. Williams describes it as "the Emperor of all birds . . . the most honourable among the feathered tribes" [56, p. 320]. It is a gentle, non-fighting creature, representative of peace and prosperity. As shown here both birds have long, graceful necks, regal crowns, and delicately suspended loose rings, giving an impression of dignity. The perfectly plain body of the upper portion of the vase is a delightful complement to the birds with detailed motif. Adding a final touch of decorative balance is the cover embellished with a leaf pattern, topped by a heart-shaped finial from which are suspended two loose rings. The general style of carving is, of course, very similar to late Ming and it is impossible to rule out the possibility that it may actually be of the earlier period. However, the ornamentation and haughty, spirited depiction of the *fêng huang* are indicative of a slightly later date. Art which emerges in a transitional period, be it jade, porcelain or any other form, is extremely difficult to date with certainty. We are compelled to rely upon our instincts to

serve as guide. Judith and Arthur Burling have written that the Chinese artist has always borne in mind, "every line or curve of an art object, or a picture, must be essential and not superfluous. To achieve 'a sense of rightness' one must feel that nothing can be added and nothing can be taken away" [4, p. 11]. This is in line with Taoist canons which dictate restraint in every endeavor. Accordingly, as we look at this vase we have the feeling that it would be an error to add or subtract anything from its composition.

Shun-chih ruled for seventeen years, and there are conflicting reports as to how he relinquished the throne. One states that he died in office. Another, that he retired to a Buddhist monastery. The latter explanation seems to be preferred. Backhouse and Bland relate that in 1661 Shun-chih became the abbot of the T'ien T'ai temple, fourteen miles to the west of Peking. "It was said . . . that the Abbot bore an extraordinary resemblance to the emperor, and to this day the temple contains a life-sized gilt mummy statue of a priest, some thirty years of age, whose features are unmistakably of the Manchu type." They further state that the Emperor K'ang-hsi visited the abbot on several occasions and the latter did not kneel to the emperor as an ordinary priest would have found it proper to do. "When, in 1670, the Abbot passed away, K'ang-hsi had a life-sized presentment of him cast in bronze, and sent presents of pearls and jewels to be buried in his tomb" [2, p. 237]. It is not possible to determine whether the story is fact or fiction, but we do know that Shun-chih was an avid Buddhist, who longed to shed the responsibilities of the cruel world in which he lived. When in his early thirties, he left the throne to his young son, K'ang-hsi, who was to be guided by a Board of Regents (government officials) until fully grown.

K'ANG-HSI   The boy of eight who ascended the throne soon displayed signs of having the strength, spirit, and intellectual capacity necessary to rule China with a firm but kindly hand. He was an enthusiastic student, painfully honest, frugal about personal expenditures, possessed an excellent memory, and true to his ancestry excelled at archery, hunting, and horsemanship. He took his responsibilities to the Chinese people seriously and, when a mere teen-ager, on seeing his regents assume too much power and greed in the management of state affairs, angrily dismissed them and undertook the full burden himself.

Gradually, he proved his good intentions to the people, particularly the scholars and literati who had doubted the Manchu purposes from the beginning. K'ang-hsi made it a practice to travel throughout the country anonymously, checking on local leaders, punishing those whom he found taking advantage of their positions to exploit the people. He issued orders to his local officials to let three characters be their guide in execution of office: *ch'ing* (purity); *shên* (carefulness); *ch'in* (diligence); thereby assuring the people that "they had officials who had been exhorted to be just" [37, p. 27]. He issued an edict stating that "all taxes unpaid on the 18th year of Shun Chih, A.D. 1661, should be remitted but that all dues accruing since that year should be gradually liquidated according to the abilities of the people, and the economic condition of each" [37, p. 33]. He ordered that land taken by the Manchus must be returned to the Chinese. He forbade the transporting of prisoners to the far north during the cold winter months. He led the army himself on more than one occasion against enemies of the state, yet in 1677 prohibited the slaughter of men in conquered territories and commanded that looting and plundering be stopped. In short, he was a leader of great integrity, firm in his convictions but constantly concerned about the fate of his people. In this regard he wrote, "The statesman can always lay the blame for his mistakes on the Sovereign, but on whom is the Sovereign to shuffle off his responsibility?

It is his bounden duty to bend his body and exhaust his energies [to diligently] care for the people'' [2, p. 259].

The court of K'ang-hsi was an enlightened one due to the fact that the emperor encouraged intellectual activity and took part in it himself. Jesuit missionaries were permitted to live in the Forbidden City for they offered new insights into science and mathematics. With the advice of Father Verbiest, the emperor completely revised the Chinese calendar, and saw to it that old books were reprinted to enrich the country's literature. Giles writes, ''His literary enterprises alone would suffice to render him illustrious'' [12, p. 360]. He supervised the compilation of the *Imperial Dictionary* with forty thousand characters, two extensive encyclopedias, historical and philosophical writings, and penned some of his own beliefs. When only sixteen years old he issued his famous *Sacred Edict,* a group of sixteen maxims outlining the proper behavior for the Chinese subject with regard to family relationships, community ethics, and responsibilities to the state. These tenets were read in every village twice a month (first and fifteenth) up to the time of the Republic of China [14, p. 38]. So this giant of a man, described by Macgowan as ''a man that could be reasoned with, but not threatened'' [32, p. 536], set the standard for the people close to him in the Forbidden City, but also saw to it that the proper moral climate was established throughout the entire country.

In traditional China, the ''social set'' was composed of the literati—the scholars who had successfully completed a very rigid set of examinations given by the state. From this group were chosen governors of provinces, of cities, and members of the governmental bureaus. Winterbotham wrote that, ''. . . the whole administration of the Chinese empire [was] entrusted to the mandarins of letters'' [57, p. 269]. The emphasis was on knowledge rather than monetary resources. Education was not only desirable but essential to achieve any position of rank. Having finished his basic studies, the scholar was expected to continue working throughout his lifetime, for it was one thing to fully digest the old philosophies, yet another to apply those principles to current problems. So the learned ruled the country, and the common man looked to the mandarin for guidance and revered him from afar.

This respect for education is still reflected in Chinese attitudes all over the world. In the United States we have the toiling laundry man whose sons are invariably college graduates. In Red China, the communists have placed a high priority on schooling for their youth, even though they have chosen to reinterpret the classics to suit their own purposes. And, of course, Mao Tse-tung is an enthusiastic and well-respected poet. In Malaysia there is considerable conflict between the Chinese and the Malays due to the fact that the Malays have been rather lackadaisical about securing an education, while the Chinese have diligently sought scholastic training. Hence, the latter have assumed a very powerful position in national affairs, particularly evident in Singapore where the Chinese are extremely prosperous. In the Republic of China they cannot build schools fast enough to accommodate the students ready to attend classes! So we can see that a sound education is still highly valued. The man of letters, then, was the ''upper crust'' or ''blue blood'' of Chinese society.

Slowly becoming convinced of K'ang-hsi's good intentions, the literati shed their belligerence and began to believe that the emperor had, indeed, accepted the Mandate of Heaven. Having won their confidence, K'ang-hsi gathered the outstanding artists of the day about him at the court and set them to work. He encouraged the arts, establishing workshops within the palace precincts. There were twenty-seven ateliers set up for imperial wares and even one designated exclusively for the manufacture of jade *ju-i* scepters. Prosperity was rampant, and creative genius responded to the abundance and carefree spirit of the time. Speaking of this golden era, Sherman E. Lee says that, ''The Manchu rulers themselves, particularly with regard to art, became more Chinese than the Chinese, forming great collections in the imperial city of Peking" [29, p. 441].

The emperor's household abounded in decorative jade objects as well as pieces designed for utilitarian purposes. Vases, bowls, wine vessels, cups, ritual vessels, girdle pendants, teapots, plates, cosmetic boxes, combs, hair ornaments, jewelry to enhance the appearance of the ladies of the court, belt buckles, baby locks to tie about a child's neck symbolizing his long stay on earth, brush pots, arm rests, water pots, jade-handled brushes, seals, etc., which outfitted the scholar's table, all took their place in the imperial palaces. Jade tokens were used as credentials, or carried by officials as proof of identification. The sonorous quality of jade was pleasing to the ear, so that carriages were hung with jade bells and slabs of nephrite were cut for use as musical instruments. Jade mortars and pestles were utilized for pounding drugs. Aside from its service at table, in the scholar's study, about the palace halls, in religious ceremonies and for use as personal adornment, carved jade in the form of *ju-i* scepters were bestowed upon distinguished citizens of the empire.

Those individuals who had achieved great honor for the emperor in literary accomplishment, artistic endeavor, prudence in exercising the law, or military heroism, were given a scepter as a lasting token of the emperor's gratitude for service well done. This practice is similar to the Western custom of awarding medals to those whom we honor. Scepters were also given to visiting dignitaries and ambassadors, and it was the custom for the groom to present his bride with a scepter on their wedding day.

The term *ju-i* means "as you wish" which is similar to our "may all your wishes come true." Its curved form with almost heart-shaped top knob is representative of the *ling chih* plant (*Polyporus ludicus*), a type of fungus native to China which is said to be the "herb of immortality" (Taoist doctrine) due to its remarkable indestructability. The gracefully curved shape is also re-garded as a stylized version of the lotus with long stem carried by Buddhist deities. According to Hansford, "the flower is supposed to enshrine the 'wish-granting jewel' *ju-i pao*" [22]. Therefore, whether your preference is for Taoist or Buddhist principles, it is safe to say that the *ju-i* scepter was intended to bestow long life and the realiza-tion of one's dreams upon the fortunate recipient (Plate 23).

We know that the three major religions as well as many traditional folkways played a large part in Chinese daily existence. Elaborate ceremonies were held at appropriate times of the year. The emperor worshiped heaven, as the sole representative of the people, exercising the Mandate of Heaven. There were seasonal sacrifices in an effort to please the supernatural creatures who provided the neces-sary elements for abundant crops. Werner states that sacrifices of animals, silk, grain, and jade were made, that "panegyrics were sung, and robes of appropriate colour worn" [54, p. 35]. Ritual vessels were carefully selected for each occasion according to function and color. For instance, red was used for the Altar to the Sun, and a very pale blue (gray cast) or white for the Altar to the Moon. As Chinese soil is yellow, this color was used in agricul-tural rites. We illustrate several jades which reflect this tradition (Plates 14, 18, and 26).

Thus we have seen that articles of jade were used for many diverse purposes in Chinese life. Jade was an in-tegral part of daily existence and so venerated that *The Book of Rites* states, "The Superior Man competes in vir-tue with Jade" [56, p. 233]. The stone has always been associated with purity. It is, therefore, not surprising to read a statement by Emperor K'ang-hsi wherein he expounds his own virtues and speaks of never erring, so as to permit "no flaw in the jade of my good name" [2]. Because of its intrinsic qualities, jade was regarded as one of the most valuable possessions. In Emperor K'ang-hsi's dictionary it is suggested that an effective remedy for robbery would be to discard jade and destroy pearls, "so that petty thieves will disappear, there being no valuables left to steal" [13].

The emperor revered jade in the true Chinese sense, and when he decided to build a summer retreat in the cool hills of the northwest at Jehol (Inner Mongolia) in 1703, the grounds surrounding the palace included the Jade Girdle Bridge, the Jade Canal, and the Jade Fountain Pagoda among other edifices of a similar nature. The old texts constantly describe the mountains and waters of the gardens as "pure" or "clear" like jade [33].

In this peaceful setting, K'ang-hsi could escape from the burdens of state, the bustle of the Peking court and take time for meditation and aesthetic pursuits. Here he was able to satisfy his taste for horseback riding and the hunt, skills which came naturally to K'ang-hsi, thanks to his Manchurian ancestry and great physical strength. The scenic mountains served as a constant inspiration for literary and other artistic endeavors (Plate 21).

The glorious reign of Emperor K'ang-hsi came to an end in 1722. He died at sixty-nine after having seen his country through many trials and triumphs for over sixty years. His standards of conduct in presiding as ruler had always been of the highest order. The Jesuit fathers wrote of him in glowing terms speaking of "his wise government, his prowess in war and sport, his deep learning, multitudinous paternity and kind heart" [2]. His accomplishments in the arts and sciences were many. In addition to the exquisite jade carvings created under his influence, the production of porcelain reached a decorative peak it had never known before.

During K'ang-hsi's administration more territory had been added to the Chinese dominion. In 1689 he had signed a treaty with Russia specifying that the country north of the Amur River belonged to Russia, and the country south of the Amur River belonged to China. There was, for once, peace in the north as well as the rest of the nation, and the people knew the joys of affluence.

For the Manchu lad had grown to maturity, and the empire with him. While there were still those who could not give their total allegiance to the "foreign" regime, they respected K'ang-hsi as a man of superior intellect and integrity. He did, after all, appreciate the literary traditions of the ancient Chinese as well as efforts of contemporaries. Poetry, painting, porcelain, jade—all the arts reflect that which came before and that which evolved therefrom in the early 18th century. Even though K'ang-hsi and his court lived well, the people were not taxed unmercifully to support the throne. Soldiers died in battle, but the emperor had taken the same risks himself on a number of occasions, and these military exploits had proven beneficial for the country. K'ang-hsi understood the importance of the smallest segment of the whole— that in unity there is strength. Yet he did not oppress the people in order to achieve his goals. He demanded adherence to moral and legal codes, but knew that man had the right to till his land and reap the hard earned bounty. Essentially, he did not ask more of his subjects than he did of himself. In a position of power and wealth it would have been easy to become self-indulgent, disinterested in the plight of others. But K'ang-hsi had a dream which spurred him on. He recognized the potential of his people, their intellectual, spiritual, and material strength. This nation would consolidate and prosper under his guidance —by his will.

His grandmother, of whom K'ang-hsi was very fond, once asked the young regent what his aims and purposes were as a king, to which he replied, "Peace in the empire and the prosperity of the people" [37, p. 23]. He died having fully realized his aspirations.

Plate 14   In the same spirit as Plate 18, but rendered with an innova-
tional, decidedly decorative eye is this yellow jade vase with dragon
and phoenix birds. Graceful in form, it is embellished with imaginative designs including the familiar *t'ao t'ieh* (ogre masks found on
ancient bronze vessels) which have somehow lost their ferocity. By
the same token, the giant dragon though a dominant figure, has a
short tail, smooth back, benign claws and a pleasant smile upon his
face. Phoenix birds which represent peace, good will and prosperity
for all, round out the joyful message. Measuring 5 inches tall, $6\frac{3}{4}$
inches long, the piece has a waxy surface and the material is delicately highlighted with brown. Dragons are depicted throughout
Chinese art in every disposition and it is typical of Chinese philosophy that no matter how dangerous or ominous a creature may be,
there is always the other side of his nature to be considered—the
meditative mood, the playful interlude, the moment of happiness.

Fogg Art Museum, Harvard University: Dane Bequest.

Plate **15**   Illustrated is a white jade dragon with a young cub on its back. Instead of the usual frantic climb upward, the familiar surging, writhing struggle, or the desperate pursuit of the "precious pearl" we have here a quiet, touching portrayal of these mythological creatures. Yet even as they rest in deep meditation their potential strength and power is evident. Note the great curved back of the larger animal, the broad forehead, bulging facial features, long streaming hairlocks, and ridged horn. The cub, whose features follow the elders' closely, seems to be moving a bit, one leg stretched taut, another clutching the side of the larger creature. There is rounded symmetry about the composition; horns, pelt, and sweeping tails all curve in a complementary manner. The entire depiction of these supernatural, much revered animals is sympathetic, affectionate. Indicative of the perfection with which carvings of this period were executed, are the carefully cut feet which appear on the bottom of the carving. It was not enough to assume or give the impression that the dragon's feet were tucked underneath. On turning the jade over one had to see positive proof. The piece is 2 3/16 inches tall, $5\frac{3}{4}$ inches long, and has a soft polish. In its non-garish, non-spectacular, highly subtle refinement this group is the very synthesis of fine K'ang-hsi jade art.

Fogg Art Museum, Harvard University: Dane Bequest.

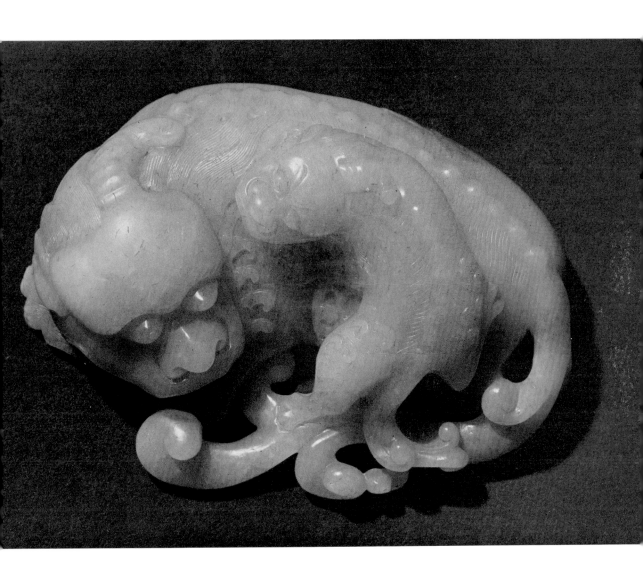

Plate 16 Depicted here is a twin fish group seemingly locked in an embrace, their curved tails entwined, fins touching, the whole resting upon waves. From their heavy, scaled bodies we assume that these are carp, which have always been common to China's waters. Carp are often depicted this way, as fish are reputed to swim in pairs, being symbolic of harmony and connubial bliss—the joys of union. The dragon heads allude to the legend that the fish of the Yellow River swim upstream periodically, and those which succeed in passing above the rapids of Lung-men are transformed into dragons; therefore, the carp represents endurance and achievement, qualities which are likened to success in literary endeavors. The flaming pearl between the two heads has a Buddhist origin and is generally considered to be "the jewel that grants every desire" [22]. We seem to have here a combination of symbols which add up to a joyous union, together with the fulfilling of ones desires and ambitions —literary scholarship being the very highest of accomplishments in China. The carving itself is gracefully executed, the creatures themselves softly, lovingly melting around one another. Even the overly exaggerated bestial heads seem to wear a humorous, warm expression accented by curled whiskers, widely innocent eyes, and snub noses. Of gray nephrite, $7\frac{1}{2}$ inches tall, the piece has that emotional appeal inherent in many K'ang-hsi jades.

Metropolitan Museum of Art: Gift of Heber R. Bishop, 1902.

Plate 17   As agriculture was the dominant industry in China, the farmer and his beasts of burden a common sight outside large cities, we often see jade carvings devoted to this subject. An excellent example is this white jade water buffalo with small boy. The reclining animal is obviously amused by the antics of his companion, as evidenced by his smiling countenance. He seems to be indulging his small friend, as the branches of millet with which the boy tickles him would not appear to be able to make a dent in that massive structure. The entire mood of the piece from the curved tail of the buffalo with its upturned tip, to the jaunty gait of the boy, is one of lighthearted warmth. Measuring approximately $7\frac{1}{4}$ inches long, the piece is cut of a soft white nephrite burnished with rust-gold touches here and there. With its "wax" surface, fully rounded composition, and gentle touch of humor, this jade manages to convey a simplicity, an unsophisticated goodness typical of Chinese rural life.

Metropolitan Museum of Art: Gift of Heber R. Bishop, 1902.

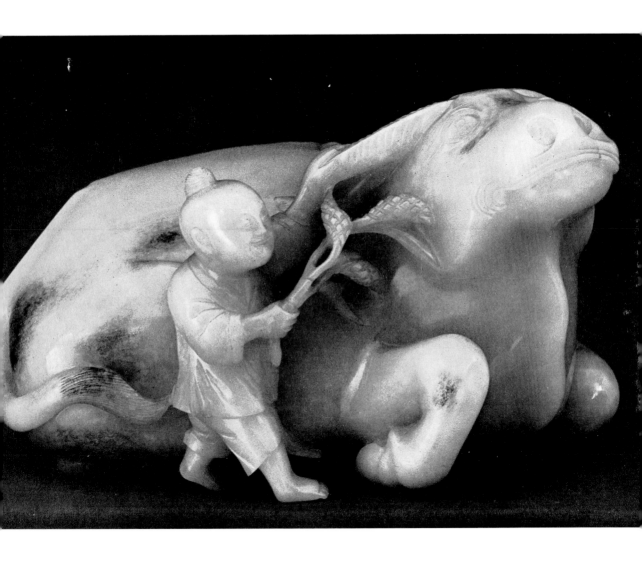

Plate 18 Illustrated is a yellow jade libation vessel presumably intended for use at the Altar of Earth or Altar to Agriculture. This carving, measuring $6\frac{1}{2}$ inches tall, is a stylized version of an ancient bronze form, its tilted stance perhaps indicative of a reaching up to the heavens for assistance. A *ch'i-lin* (Kylin) sometimes called the Chinese unicorn, sweeps around from the back of the vessel and vigorously scales the height of the vase, its curved claws clutching the wall, its eyes open, intent upon its task. The various spiral decorations are archaic thunder-cloud motifs, while the top rim is cut with a traditional key-pattern banding which represents thunder or the advent of rain. The boldly cut handle is in the form of a *k'uei*, the spiritual dragon which produces wind and rain to benefit mankind. So we have a composition which incorporates various pictographic symbols and mythological creatures, executed in a most dignified manner, for the purpose of insuring the appropriate weather conducive to abundant crops. Its substantial bulk, gracefully curving symmetry and enormous vitality bring to mind Laufer's comment that "The works of the past are copied, not slavishly and languidly, but with a zealous and fervent inspiration, with an honest desire to produce the best, with a truly artistic instinct" [28].

Metropolitan Museum of Art: Gift of Heber R. Bishop, 1902.

Plate 19 Belonging in the same group as Plate 14 is this gray-green jade vessel with brown shadings, which measures 6½ inches tall and has three dragons cut in high relief. The animals strain upward, two of them having reached the top holding on in taut silence, their eyes bulging, a flaming pearl alongside. In addition to the *t'ao-t'ieh* which decorates the front of this libation ewer, cut in almost full round is a bowl which stands upon a three-tiered pedestal. This last appears almost as an incidental addition to the whole, its significance not clear. There is no mistaking the meticulous carving, namely, the adherence to "antique" themes, and the soft, smooth surface texture of the stone. These characteristics easily place this example in the K'ang-hsi period.

M. H. de Young Memorial Museum: Avery Brundage Collection.

Plate 20   A white jade bronze-form vase, measuring 8 inches tall, has a sharply squared shape softened by swirling waves and rockery from which cloud formations and dragons emerge. Their climb is ever upward from the depths of the angry sea in pursuit of the "precious pearl" (see Plate 22). The key-pattern banding on cover and edge is adopted from the ancient pictographic symbol for clouds and thunder. Just below, the circle with three curlicues and central dot known as *yüan wo* is emblematic of nourishment. Beneath this appears a series of leaf patterns containing geometric motifs, and the major banding features a *t'ao-t'ieh* mask. The designs are borrowed once again from Shang and Chou bronzes in the hope that enlistment of the spiritual symbols and creatures of the universe will produce the elements necessary for abundant crops. The artist has here expressed an ancient theme, incorporating traditional motifs, but his style and over-all format are uniquely of the K'ang-hsi era.

Newark Museum.

Plate 21   Many mountain carvings of jade have been passed on to us from the K'ang-hsi and later periods. Here we have a white nephrite mountain, $14\frac{1}{2}$ inches long, 8 inches tall, depicting a scholar or artist riding an ox, his servant close behind. In the distance is a robed figure, perhaps a monk, waiting to greet his visitors. The traveler seems close to his destination and anxious to cover the last lap of his journey as he bends over the rapidly striding animal. He has probably come to this pastoral place seeking solitude for study. It was common practice for the artist to spend time in the country, meditating upon the wonders of nature, the Taoist way, then returning to his studio to interpret his impressions. Similarly, this jade mountain has a storybook quality, a touch of romance as if the artist, having savored the flavor of trees and hills, sat in his workshop once more and created the quaint figures, swaying trees, layered rockery and small, twin-peaked structure at the top from memory.

The design shows an excellent sense of balance. A group of trees and men on the right is set off by a clump of trees at the left; a structure is complemented by a tree at bottom center and a single figure is diagonally set off by the beast and rider. The small bridge provides a smooth plain to break up a complicated picture, and all these elements set against the huge mountain structure are well spaced. There is no overcrowding. One is impressed with the overwhelming power of nature's creation and man's place in the cosmic realm. The pine trees depicted in several places symbolize friendship and successful scholarship, while the mulberry at the extreme right is an emblem of sublime attainment and was pointed out as a sign of peace by the great philosopher, Mencius.

Here, in this one jade mountain, is embodied the Chinese love of nature reflected in Taoist thought, and their desire to seek refuge in the quiet tranquillity of the country, to take time for contemplation of the mysteries of life. Looking at such a mountain Una Pope-Hennessey wrote, "We may apprehend how deeply the love of nature . . . penetrated the Chinese heart" [44].

M. H. de Young Memorial Museum: Avery Brundage Collection.

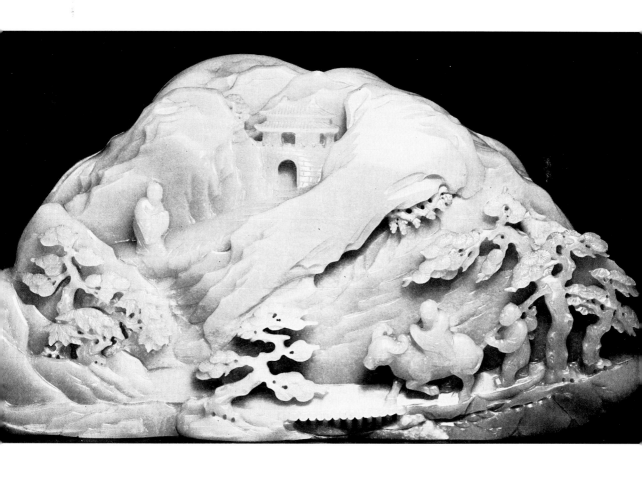

Plate 22   A white nephrite beaker-form vase, measuring $9\frac{3}{4}$ inches tall, has rounded corners and is cut in high relief. At the base and running up the side are sinuously portrayed dragons. The dominant figure of the traditional dragon (*lung*) at top right, with scaly back, four-clawed feet, heavy beard and long lash of a tail, adds impact to the theme, "dragons in pursuit of pearls." His chin rests on the lip of the vase, as he clutches the wall for balance, his body straining to gain control. The "precious pearl" with accompanying fiery or mystical rays is a very common motif which has been given various interpretations. It is identified with the sun and moon, as well as the natural pearl. Hansford states that the dragon as "Lord of the Waters" possessed pearls as he would other riches of the sea [22]. Williams refers to the analogy of the Chinese dragon to the alligator which emerges from hibernation in the spring "when the dragon is believed to be exerting its beneficient influence."

From the *Shuo Wén* dictionary (A.D. 100) we learn that, "In the spring [the dragon] ascends to the skies and in autumn it buries itself in the watery depths" [56]. He is the symbol of spring rain when nature once again gathers strength for growth and, therefore, promises an ample harvest. The dragons on this beaker, then, are rising up from their watery winter habitat to inaugurate the spring season. Again, we are reminded that the earth provided prosperity or ruin, its produce dependent upon the seasons, the seasons dictated by the spiritual beings which ruled the universe. An outmoded belief? Perhaps. Yet the specter of hunger looms large even today, and many an Asian seeks the comfort of the beneficient dragon to insure a plentiful harvest.

Metropolitan Museum of Art: Gift of Heber R. Bishop, 1902.

Plate *23*   Of particular rarity is this white jade scepter dedicated to the Emperor K'ang-hsi himself. Measuring 18 inches long, the top or broad shield of the scepter is decorated with a bat (*fu-i*) denoting long life and happiness, under which appears the character *shou* also signifying longevity, which is flanked on either side by *fêng huang* (phoenix) birds denoting an auspicious occasion. On the stem or body of the handle are several sets of calligraphy which were translated in the original Bishop books and are included herewith. Directly under the shield are two characters which read *Yu chih* meaning "Made at the Imperial Manufactory." Below this, in the center, are two vertical lines which read: *Ching yuan lou fêng nien* | *T'ien hsia hsien ju-i* meaning, "With reverential vows for a succession of fertile years, and that throughout the world every wish be fulfilled!" And finally there appears the words *Ch'en Wu Ching kung chin* meaning "Respectfully presented [to the emperor] by his servant Wu Ching" [3, Vol. II, No. 446]. The tri-lobed end which completes the piece is carved with a bat having a fillet and swastika suspended from its mouth, a peony blossom tied on either side. As stated above, the bat signifies long life. The swastika is emblematic of Buddha's heart and the peony represents riches and honors. In fashioning this scepter for Emperor K'ang-hsi, the artist carefully selected the appropriate symbols and sentiments to wish his leader long years of happiness and prosperity. It was the custom during the Manchu control, to place a *ju-i* scepter on a table in front of the throne in each of the palace reception rooms, which is most probably the purpose for which this *ju-i* was intended. We sometimes see these scepters made of carved wood or lacquer, inset with three jade plaques. However, their fussy, ornate frames usually detract from the beauty of the jade, and cannot be favorably compared to the quiet charm and innate dignity evident here.

Metropolitan Museum of Art: Gift of Heber R. Bishop, 1902.

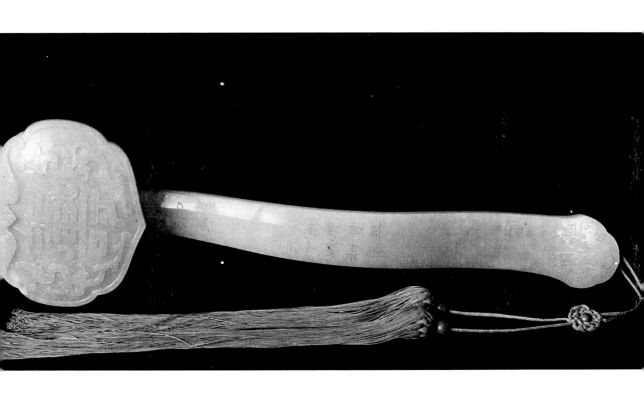

Plate 24　The elegance of the K'ang-hsi era is personified in a spinach jade double-gourd vase measuring 10 inches tall, 5¼ inches wide (at the fullest part of lower section). Multiple leaves, flowers, and gourd fruits are deftly cut in profusion all over the surface of the vase, and the form is further accented by two leaf-covered handles bearing a loose ring each. The decoration is symbolic of a long, contented life blessed with many children. Though there is virtually no polish on the vase, the even dark green color of the material imparts an opulent flavor to the composition. This is a very beautiful K'ang-hsi piece; a forerunner of the precise and highly creative jades which appeared in the late 18th century.

Fogg Art Museum, Harvard University: Dane Bequest.

YUNG-CHENG   K'ang-hsi had deliberated carefully about his successor to the throne. Finally, on his deathbed, he selected Yung-cheng, his fourth son, to rule the empire. He was obviously not a very ingratiating fellow, as history records his brothers bore him great resentment and continually plotted his downfall. As so often happens, the new monarch was not the "giant" his father had been. He spent a good part of his time dealing out punishments to his brothers, and managed to earn the animosity of several religious groups in the country. His literary accomplishments, though numerous, are chiefly concerned with glorious accounts of his own personal triumphs. Fortunately, Yung-cheng reigned for just twelve years, from 1723 to 1735.

Thus Yung-cheng is not remembered with any great reverence. He managed to antagonize the Buddhist factions in the country, resulting in numerous uprisings in his brief reign, and he openly persecuted the Christians; first banishing the Jesuits to Canton and then sending them out of the country to Macao in 1732. This small area was a trading mecca for the Portuguese but existed under strict Chinese domination. Yung-cheng's enemies were many, which probably accounts for the discrepancy in the reports of the manner in which he died; some historians stating that he was murdered, others that he reached his deathbed as a result of illness. In any case, he obligingly bequeathed the "Mandate of Heaven" to his fourth son, Ch'ien-lung, who was destined to be one of the most celebrated and well-respected rulers China had ever known.

Again we are faced with the problem of dating. Yung-cheng occupied the throne for so short a time that it is exceedingly difficult to assign jade carvings to his reign with any assurance. As far as we know, jade production continued without interruption, but the general appearance of the pieces remains about the same.

Plate 25
(See overleaf)

A white jade water jar measuring $6\frac{3}{4}$ inches long is attributed to the Yung-cheng period. Though rather crudely executed, it has a definite charm. The vessel itself is perfectly plain, serving to enhance the loose rings which hang from tiger-head handles. The ferocious tiger is lord of all wild animals, king of beasts, who wards off evil spirits and protects one from harm. He presumably lives to a thousand years of age. These concepts are also carried out in the depiction of the *ling chih* (herb of immortality) plants at the bottom, and the artemisia leaf which protects one from physical harm. The owner of this jar was to live a long life in safety.

Metropolitan Museum of Art: Gift of Heber R. Bishop, 1902.

Plate 26
(Facing page)

This yellow jade libation vessel, $6\frac{1}{2}$ inches tall, is attributed to the Yung-cheng period [41, p. 179]. A powerfully executed dragon head holds the bulk of the vessel in its wide-open mouth, the eyes bulging in herculean effort, the whiskers tensely curved back, the animal's full strength set upon its task. Clutching the smooth surface above are two *ch'ih lung* (archaic dragons) which hark back to traditional bronze decoration. The pale yellow material signifying earth, and the dragon rising up from the water are indications that the piece is in keeping with those made for use in agricultural rites. Although baroque in shape, it exhibits a definite sense of balance and has a pleasing, sensitive surface or tactile quality.

Norton Gallery of Art: Stanley Charles Nott Collection.

The new monarch was twenty-five years old when he ascended the throne, and is described as a powerful man whose nature was much like that of his grandfather, K'ang-hsi. He was a wise and able statesman who took his responsibility to the people very seriously, and pledged himself to the security and welfare of the nation. His armies reached out to acquire more territory for the empire. During his reign Mongolia was held in control; Chinese Turkestan was placed under Chinese dominion; Tibet gave in to Chinese strength; Nepal and Burma, having invaded Tibetan territory, were forced to pay tribute to China, as were Annam, Korea, Afghanistan, and Russian Turkestan. Not since the Yuan dynasty had the emperor of China ruled over such a vast empire [33]. Latourette describes Ch'ien-lung as, "the equal of the two most famous monarchs of the Europe of his day, Catherine of Russia and Frederich of Prussia, and in the wealth and population of his realm he surpassed all other contemporary rulers" [27]. To balance this imposing portrait, we are told that Ch'ien-lung possessed a creative mind which manifested itself in poetic accomplishment, and an enthusiasm for artistic endeavor of all kinds. Soothill states that, "Belles-lettres, art, architecture, the arts, industry, trade, agriculture, administration, education, all prospered during this glorious reign" [50].

The empire was secure under Ch'ien-lung. Foreign trade flourished. Silk, porcelain, and tea were the most popular exports. Twenty million pounds of tea were exported each year during his reign, and the wealth poured in. At that time, China was the only country that grew tea leaves. There was very little exchange of trade with Europe, as the Chinese needed nothing from the "foreign barbarians." So the economy was strong. It was not until the late 19th century when the English offered opium for Chinese consumption, that much reciprocal trade commenced and actually served to hasten the downfall of the Manchus.

A painting of the Emperor Ch'ien-lung by W. Alexander, a member of the British Embassy to China led by Lord Macartney, portrays him wearing elaborate silk robes embroidered with imperial dragon designs, pointed high boots, and peaked hat. His jewelry consists of a long mandarin bead necklace and an archer's ring on each thumb. The beads and rings are probably jade. In addition to the wearing of jade jewelry, the emperor surrounded himself with fine art throughout his apartments. From the writings of Attiret, a Jesuit artist at the court, we learn that the emperor had, "brought together everything which art and good taste [could] add to the riches of nature" [33]. He was not only conscious of native art, but delighted in the innovations which European designs offered. His pavilion in imitation of Versailles was widely admired, and he had a large collection of European watches and clocks. Van Braam, a Dutch-American member of the embassy of the Dutch East India Company wrote in 1795 of the imperial library lined with shelves: "on which are collected all the most valuable and scarce Chinese productions, consisting both of precious stones and antiques" [33].

Just as the emperor combed the country for lost manuscripts and had them copied for the imperial library by the best calligraphers available, he likewise encouraged detection of all kinds of fine art. Bushell related the story of a very large jade wine bowl, some $4\frac{1}{2}$ feet tall (other accounts state 2 feet tall) which graced the Khan's palace during Mongol rule (Yuan dynasty, 14th century) [30, p. 102; 44, p. 46]. Friar Oderick, who visited Peking in 1318, said the vessel was, "of a certain stone called Merdacas . . . so fine [that] its price exceeded the value of four great towns." He goes on to describe the carving of fierce dragons embellished with gold and "fringes of network of great pearls." Originally pipelines brought drink from a central source keeping the bowl full, and golden goblets were placed alongside in readiness to quench the royal thirst. The bowl disappeared after the fall of the Mongol reign, only to turn up again during the

18th century, devoid of jewels, in the kitchen of a poor Buddhist temple where it was being used as a container for salted vegetables! Emperor Ch'ien-lung purchased it for a few hundred ounces of silver, composed a poem which was engraved on the inside of the vessel, and brought it back to its regal habitat [6, Vol. I, p. 132]. A detailed description of this bowl and the circumstances surrounding its return to imperial quarters is inscribed on a jade tablet in the Chester Beatty Library, as dictated by Emperor Ch'ien-lung himself [53, p. 20].

The emperor was given first choice of the boulders of rough jade which were transported by camel from Yarkand to Peking, as he frequently commissioned the finest workshops to make certain pieces for him from the carefully selected rough. This practice had been maintained for hundreds of years. The Jesuit, Benedict Goes, en route to Peking at the request of Matteo Ricci during the Ming dynasty was delayed in Yarkand (Turkestan) and had the opportunity of studying the principle commerce of the land. Una Pope-Hennessy states that Goes "was told that all the jade consigned from Yarkand to China had on arrival to be submitted to the inspection of the Emperor of Cathay, and only after he had made his choice was it permitted to dispose of the remainder by private treaty." Another story related by the same author is the meeting of Goes with the sister of the king of Kashgar whose son was Lord of Khotan (the capital of Yarkand). Both Goes and the princess were headed for Yarkand, but the princess was in dire need of funds. Goes obliged by loaning her six hundred pieces of gold. On reaching her destination, the princess paid Goes. "She chose to bestow . . . the most profitable merchandise it was possible to convey to China —jade, the hard stone so highly esteemed among the Chinese that if of purest quality it was worth more than fine gold" [44, p. 50].

Reference was made to the fact that jadeite material from Burma was not brought into China until the end of the Ch'ien-lung period. It is extremely difficult to ascertain whether a jadeite carving is actually late 18th century or of a more modern vintage. Workmanship is a key factor in determining the date of a particular piece. Modern jade carvings have a tendency to be carelessly carved and too brilliantly polished. They have a manufactured, commercial appearance which distinguishes them from works of the earlier period. Most of the jadeite carvings on the market today, and in our museums, are 19th century or later.

Although Ch'ien-lung tried very hard to follow the frugal example of his grandfather, K'ang-hsi, he seems to have had great difficulty in curbing his tastes for fine art. His writings abound with praise for economy in daily living, and apologies for personal extravagance. He verbally deplored lavish expenditures but savored the good things in life. Backhouse and Bland describe his nature thus: "There was nothing of the Puritan about him, nor of the abstainer; he loved a pretty woman and a good dinner, but held the oriental faith, that both were gifts of the gods, not to be easily won, nor lightly esteemed" [2]. In his enthusiasm for beauty, Ch'ien-lung expanded the gardens and enriched the appointments of the summer palaces which were located northwest of Peking. Many of our most beautiful examples in jade are reputed to be from an imperial summer palace (Plates 31 and 36).

Ch'ien-lung tried to share the fruits of his good fortune with those around him. Theatrical productions were shown in the Park of Universal Joy within the palace enclave. To further enhance the New Year festivities, Ch'ien-lung had booths erected in the gardens to resemble a country fair. Ladies and gentlemen of his court were invited to partake of the delicacies offered by small restaurants, wine taverns, and teahouses, in between shopping for souvenirs of porcelain, embroidery, silk, jade, and so forth. The color and animation of this scene must have gratified the emperor, whose enthusiasm for the sheer joy of living was insatiable [2, p. 335].

This was an age of creative freedom, a flamboyant, extravagant era. Hence, Ch'ien-lung jades often exhibit an overembellishment, a tendency to fill every space with pattern as in early bronze work. We find this characteristic in Ch'ien-lung porcelain too, which has the added factor of brilliant, sometimes garish color. And it shows up in other art forms such as lacquer and cloisonné. Apparently, in an effort to outdo what had already been done, the Ch'ien-lung artist frequently lost sight of good taste. Lavish designs do not always displease the aesthetic senses, however, as is the case with the truly stunning white jade libation vessel (Plate 35) and the white jade dragon bottle (Plate 36).

There is a definite lack of continuity in the decorative motif or theme of quite a few Ch'ien-lung jades. The emphasis was placed on artistic merit, creative genius, and technical skill, rather than on significant meaning. Laufer wrote that, "The old-time rigid sacredness was redeemed by a more human and social touch . . . the subjects were still drawn from the ancient sources, but with a predilection for the genre" [28] (Plates 39 and 40).

It is well to stress once more that jade objects were employed for many different purposes. Jade took its place at the table, on the person, in the ceremonial halls and at religious rites. From the imperial court down to the poorest farmer, jade was revered as a substance of value and purity. The Chinese employed in the most menial task treasured his small bit of jade (as today the poorest fisherwoman in Hong Kong wears her jade bangle while attending to daily chores). Of course, the wealthy citizen owned the finest examples, and the emperor's personal collection contained the cream of the jade carver's crop.

Emperor Ch'ien-lung ruled for sixty years. At the age of eighty-five, though in good health, he decided to abdicate in favor of his son, Chia-ch'ing. There were several reasons for his decision which offer a rare insight into the Chinese mind. First of all, his revered grandfather, K'ang-hsi, had reigned for sixty-one years and it would have been unseemly for his grandson to outdo him. Secondly, the

Chinese calendar is computed over a sixty-year period, the twelve terrestrial branches (animals of the zodiac) and ten celestial stems (natural elements) being combined in consecutive order five times to complete the cycle of sixty. Therefore, it is quite possible that Ch'ien-lung felt it an honor to have been permitted to rule for a complete cycle and an affront to the gods to consider a longer reign. As an added determinant Ch'ien-lung found signs of import from Heaven. He took heed of the fact that on New Year's day of the sixtieth year of his reign an eclipse of the sun was due. On the following Festival of Lanterns (first moon, fifteenth day) there would be a lunar eclipse. He stated, "Heaven sends these portents as warnings, but a Sovereign's duty is to be guided by his conscience and to be aware of his shortcomings at all times, so that an eclipse is not needed to awaken him to a sense of duty" [2].

He relinquished the throne after having served the people and nation well. During his rule territory had been added to the empire, and conservation had been effected along the Yellow River. The country was wealthy. He had been responsible for the publication of many heretofore unheralded literary works, and had seen to it that the classics were revised and reissued. A descriptive catalogue of the contents of the imperial library had been published containing 3,460 works in the categories of classics, history, philosophy, and general literature [12]. He was a statesman, historian, poet, and warm human being. Never again was China to have as able and conscientious an administrator, whose enthusiasm and encouragement had fostered the creation of superbly executed, magnificent works of art; art which Burwell refers to as "an apex of perfection and refinement never touched before or since" [5].

Plate 27 Pictured is a sage green brush holder of imposing size, 8 inches in diameter, the exterior of which is cut in deep relief depicting a profusion of figures amid foliage and rockery. The rich green and rust-spot tones highlight a fully developed landscape scene known to the Chinese as the "Orchid Pavilion." Here man has the opportunity to pursue his own interests; painting, calligraphy, poetry, and quiet meditation are his prerogative. There is movement in the swirling water, but the trees stand still, and the figures sit upon jagged cut rocks which seem suspended in space. The mind is active, the body functioning, the universe continuing on its inevitable course, yet here time matters not, as man, through nature, seeks the Tao—the way!

Metropolitan Museum of Art: Gift of Heber R. Bishop, 1902.

Plate 28 This white jade jar with cover, measuring $14\frac{5}{8}$ inches tall, speaks
eloquently of the lavish, exciting time from which it emanates.
Reflected in the pure white jade is the old and the new, done with
the genius of the fully developed medium. The shape of the vase is
modern and quite graceful. Reticulated bird-form knobs embellish
the plain neck, and loose rings are appended to similar archaic
bird heads. The ancient *t'ao t'ieh* (ogre mask) motif appears as the
main design on the body of the vase, surrounded by geometric patterns. The cover has a band of this pattern too, but its full blown
peony finial breaks the sober mood. Here we have traditional subjects interpreted with an ornamental eye, yet tempered with a keen
sense of balance; in its entirety, a tribute to the skill and good taste
indicative of better examples of this period.

Minneapolis Institute of Arts: Gift of Augustus L. Searle.

Plate **29** A fine white jade brush washer in the shape of a double gourd which measures 3 inches tall, 9 inches long, $4\frac{3}{4}$ inches in diameter, is delicately carved with a supple yet precise touch. The bat appears to float on his perch, and the lightly veined leaves play softly on the surface of the fruit of the plant. There is a fairyland quality about this piece, its symbolism clearly shown in the choice of the gourd form and the bat decoration; the former containing many seeds which guarantee innumerable progeny and the latter insuring long life; the whole a fitting accouterment to the scholar's table.

Minneapolis Institute of Arts: Gift of Mr. and Mrs. Augustus L. Searle.

Plate 30   A square white jade water pot stands $4\frac{7}{8}$ inches tall and shows the remarkable dexterity of which the lapidary was capable. The top strip, probably intended for use as a brush rest, consists of a plain bar with a dragon firmly coiled about its length; the scaly body, beard, horns, and sweeping tail vigorously represent the beast. Phoenix birds with regal crowns form two handles, their deftly patterned wing plumage and curled tail feathers an elegant exercise in symmetry. On each side of the body of the vessel are carved four of the Eight Immortals (Pa Hsien) in a forest scene with appropriate foliage and rockery. Here we have a very distinctive composition, incorporating the old symbols in an original manner.

Seattle Art Museum: Eugene Fuller Memorial Collection.

Plate 31   A white jade vase measuring 12¾ inches tall, reputedly once kept in the Summer Palace, has borders and base embellished with a steady key-fretwork motif. The cover bears similar key fretwork and is surmounted by a crouching dragon. Loose rings are suspended from finely cut elephant-head handles, their thick, wrinkled trunks and heavily browed eyes bespeaking the sturdy structure of this powerful animal which symbolizes long life. The front and back of the vase are decorated with four of the Eight Buddhist Symbols centering a stylized version of the *shou* (symbol of longevity). The sides are carved with palm trees and flying storks, the former representing retirement. Again, this vase embodies traditional ideology with a modern viewpoint.

Metropolitan Museum of Art: Gift of Heber R. Bishop, 1902.

Plate 32   A white jade vase 11¼ inches tall, displays clean, simple lines, precisely cut decoration, and broad areas of blank space. The bronze-form vessel has key-pattern banding on the edge of the cover and lip, a row of highly stylized recumbent silkworms, a delicately cut *t'ao t'ieh* mask set against an interlocked "T" ground, and a series of leaf emblems just above the plain foot of the vase. Notice that the *t'ao t'ieh* is actually constructed of silkworm emblems and *ju-i* heads, while the large flaring scroll designs which appear on either side of the mask incorporate the same symbols plus the *yüan wo* (nourishment). This central motif is exceedingly graceful and imaginative. Two *ju-i* scepter handles in the traditional *ling chih* form add further balance to the composition and hold a loose ring each. Here we have the desire for a long life of plenty. The primitive, crude hand is gone. Technical know-how and aesthetic judgment have been combined to produce a work of utmost refinement.

Newark Museum.

Plate 33 One of the most striking and superb examples of the lapidary's genius is this rust brown-and-white vase which stands $11\frac{5}{8}$ inches tall. Here is a tribute to what Ashton & Grey call the Chinese carver's "great sense of material" [1]. The pronounced design has been cut from the outer brown shell of the jade rough, thereby achieving a "cameo" effect which contrasts beautifully with the clean white background. Two archaic dragons surmount the cover bearing touches of brown and sporting a loose ring each. The key-pattern rim of cover, vase, and foot are cut in brown, as is the large *shou* (symbol of longevity) which is the main theme of the vase. A pair of confronted dragons joyfully touching another *shou* emblem form the major design of the vessel. The dragons have been fashioned in a geometrically squared style to conform with the shape of the vase. While the motif and form of this piece are traditional in feeling, through the skillful use of material and a modern rendering of ancient symbols, the work emerges as a fresh, thoroughly satisfying artistic achievement!

Walker Art Center, Minneapolis.

Plate 34   Another attractive example with color properties similar to the preceding is this winged chimera. Again, the material is used advantageously but in a different manner. Here the lapidary has incorporated the deep brown color into the body of the composition, giving the lion its own ''pedigree'' marks. The animal sits with tail curled tight, feet planted firmly, head erect, eyes alert, mouth open displaying ominously sharp teeth—the epitome of canine strength! This mythological creature, made of stone in massive sizes, was placed in front of graves from the Han dynasty on and was expected to deter any evildoers. The subject representation measures only $5\frac{1}{2}$ inches tall, $3\frac{1}{2}$ inches wide, but manages to impart the fiery virility of its illustrious ancestor.

M. H. de Young Memorial Museum: Avery Brundage Collection.

Plate 35   A white jade libation vessel measures 14 inches long, 10 inches tall. The basic shape is borrowed from an old bronze form and sumptuously covered with flowers cut in high relief. This decoration extends to right and left of the central body of the piece, in the form of birds and foliage cut with exquisite precision. The cover is surmounted by graceful *fêng huang* birds, their splayed tail feathers falling softly on clean ground. This magnificent exercise in design shows complete control of the material, which has been skillfully utilized to create a uniquely beautiful work of art.

American Museum of Natural History: William Boyce Thompson Collection.

Plate 36   Another richly bedecked example is this white jade dragon bottle (cover missing) presumably from the Summer Palace. Measuring $10\frac{3}{4}$ inches tall, the pilgrim vase shown boasts a curvy, sinuous, scaled dragon on each shoulder busily employed in support of the lip. On the front panel, carved in a great burst of exuberance, is a ferocious representation of an imperial five-clawed dragon (*kan-chu lung*) with flaring whiskers, cunning eyes, and gaping full-toothed mouth. His body twists and turns, writhing in activity, amidst swirls of clouds, in frenzied pursuit of the "precious pearl." Though the design is extravagant, we cannot deny its innate virility. Years ago, Alan Priest drew a poetic simile between the jades in the Bishop Collection (Metropolitan Museum of Art) and the Russian ballet, when he said that the former are, "a holiday comparable to when Nijinsky and Karsarvina and Pavlova were weaving their marvelous patterns before our inspired eyes, but in the jades the excitement is caught and frozen for all time" [46].

Metropolitan Museum of Art: Gift of Heber R. Bishop, 1902.

Plate 37　The wonderful thing about Ch'ien-lung jade is the infinite variety of style. As a contrast to the highly ornamental vase just described, we have a white jade bowl which derives its elegance from the very simplicity of its form and dearth of decoration. The bowl, cut in a semi-scalloped ovoid shape, measures $11\frac{5}{8}$ inches from handle to handle. The material is of the purest white color and is polished to a high sheen which further enhances the natural quality of the stone. Lotus handles are the only adornment on the bowl, adding a complementary note to the perfectly plain body and providing a definite balance for the elongated shape. The artisan most probably chose the lotus in association with the faultlessness of this jade material, as the flower symbolizes purity and perfection, "because it grows out of mud but is not defiled" [56]. It also contains seeds and therefore brings wishes for numerous offspring.

　　Thus it is likely that this piece was intended as a marriage bowl. The institute's *Bulletin* of April, 1932 states that the bowl was from the collection of the late boy-emperor, Hsuan-t'ung, who deposited this and other jades in the Salt Bank of Peking as collateral against loans. Unfortunately, the interest on the loans grew so high that he was never able to recover the jades, and eventually they were sold to various dealers in Tientsin by a Manchu warlord. It would probably be difficult to substantiate this tale, but the bowl is certainly of imperial quality; the original white jade boulder is of sufficient rarity to have been chosen by Ch'ien-lung himself for personal use.

Minneapolis Institute of Arts: Gift of Augustus L. Searle.

Plate 38 Dynamic in impact is this moss green jade pilgrim vase with explosive "sunburst" decoration. The vase, measuring $15\frac{1}{2}$ inches tall and $9\frac{1}{2}$ inches wide (across center) is effectively embellished with stylized *ju-i* symbols which surround a blooming peony flower, the emblem of good fortune. Toward the outer edge of the body design, situated between the *ju-i,* are the Eight Buddhist Symbols or auspicious signs. The cover is surmounted by an entwined dragon, and the fully developed dragon-head handles hold a loose ring each. Geometric banding trims the rim of cover and vase, plus the foot. While the combination of iconography is confusing, from an aesthetic standpoint the piece is very pleasing.

M. H. de Young Memorial Museum: Avery Brundage Collection.

Plate 39   This spinach jade *hu* (a vase whose shape is derived from an early bronze form), measuring 18 inches tall, is a copy of a bronze wine container, and bears many of the ancient symbols. The top rim of the vessel has key or geometric forms called *chiao-yeh*. The body of the *hu* has recumbent silkworm banding, and the main design consists of a key-fretwork ground emphasizing a broad *t'ao t'ieh* mask which is reputed to ward off greedy mouths from food vessels, although its real significance still evades us. The *t'ao t'ieh* is one of the oldest pictographs to be found in Chinese art, and is often seen on Shang bronzes. While the various subjects are depicted with a modern interpretation, the mood of the vase, its distinguished appearance, the polished but not garishly shining surface, the apparent restraint of the carefully cut decoration is true to the original bronze mood. Appropriate to this discussion, Laufer wrote of the Chinese copyist, "His work is creative reinvention, not purely receptive, but partaking of the spirit permeating the soul of the master" [28]. So again, we must give full credit to the Ch'ien-lung artisans who captured the spirit of the old in the guise of the new.

M. H. de Young Memorial Museum: Avery Brundage Collection.

Plate 40   The large bronze-form vessel is a copy of a bronze *kuei* (vessel) which was used to hold grain during ritual ceremonies. This massive piece, measuring 16 inches across the handles, $10\frac{1}{4}$ inches tall, is cut of a dark olive green jade, the material a lively, even color. Following the traditional bronze style, the design is repeated in four separate quarters, which are clearly divided by flanges (vertical ridged lines). Animals appear on the upper part of the vessel beneath the top lip in an archaic form. The four frantically twisting dragons on the main body of the *kuei* bear a close resemblance to the *k'uei lung* of early bronzes, but their long spiral tails are a modern touch. The background design is the familiar key-pattern motif. Powerful dragon handles and heavy loose rings add perfect balance to the whole, retaining the archaic form but showing a fresh interpretation. A Ch'ien-lung reign mark appears underfoot.

Smithsonian Institution: Maude Monell Vetlesen Collection.

Plate 41 Attributed to the Ch'ien-lung period is this jadeite incense burner. Measuring 6 inches tall, its most impressive features are a vivid green finial surmounting the cover, and the play of sharp green-and-white color which runs through the entire work. Carving seems secondary when one is confronted with such magnificent color. A second look, however, reveals well-detailed cutting and a pleasing symmetry to the design. Elaborate *t'ao t'ieh* masks decorate the cover and bulbous body, surrounded by sweeping scrolls and stylized interpretations of ancient pictographs. An entwined dragon garnishes the finial, and fancifully carved dragonheads form handles from which loose rings are suspended. The detail indicates a sure hand and a high, but not glaring, polish. It is just this combination of skill, refinement, and originality which distinguishes this incense burner from more recent examples and places it in the late 18th century.

Cleveland Museum of Art: Bequest of John L. Severance, 1936.

Plate 42   Another jade carving which takes its form from an ancient bronze is this covered libation vessel. The *kuang* was made in bronze to be used for heating wine or mixing the same with water. The Smithsonian's jade *kuang* is 9 inches long and is fashioned of a lively moss green material which oddly enough fits the mood of the piece. Despite the grotesque monster head, intricately entangled dragon finial, and spiny dragon handle, it is indicative of what Willetts terms the Chinese bronze sculptors' "obsession with animals," [55] while conveying the "impression of a spirit that is almost barbaric," the piece has a humorous aspect. The key-fretwork lips, *ju-i* motif amidst curling swirls on the broad band of the body, four pudgy feet, and single loose ring are all poetic interpretations of the ancient symbols. The designer has retained some of the sobriety of the early subject, but there is, nevertheless, a rambunctious quality about it all. One somehow expects those four stubby legs to gallop away with their top-heavy load!

Smithsonian Institution: Maude Monell Vetlesen Collection.

Plate 43   This spinach green jade pitcher, which has no actual bronze-form
counterpart, is reminiscent of the ancient designs in its massive
structure and choice of motif. An inverted monster head emits the
curved spout from its mouth. The ridged cover is topped by an
elaborately executed dragon and the solid bands on the body are
interspersed with flamboyantly cut representations of the eight
Buddhist symbols. The vessel measures $15\frac{5}{8}$ inches tall and is cata-
logued by Nott as a wine-distilling jar from the temple of Emperor
Ch'ien-lung in the Winter Palace, used to hold wine for rituals to
the God of Soil and Grain, or the God of Agriculture [39].

Smithsonian Institution: Maude Monell Vetlesen Collection.

Plate 44   Carved in the antique taste, and suggestive of a bronze form, the vessel opposite is of a dull gray-green nephrite, the broad side of which is a warm rust brown. The material and general appearance of this piece indicate an earlier dating (possibly late Ming) but an inscription on the base, supposedly composed by Emperor Ch'ien-lung himself, dated 1785, dictates the later attribution. Mr. Clarence Shangraw, assistant curator of the Brundage Collection, has translated the poem as follows:

> In a Khotan river it has passed a thousand autumns,
> Water-vapors and earth-trappings have not imbued it.
> Viewing it, we reject the present and recall the past,
> Singing the praises of this *ch'iu,* we must admit it's like
>   a Han vessel.
> > —Verse written by the hand of the Ch'ien-lung Emperor,
> >   in the middle of the spring of the year 1785.

There is always a possibility that the piece is actually of earlier origin, the emperor having acquired it for his collection at this late date and inscribing it as stated above. Having no proof to this effect, however, we must place it in the late 18th century, and assume that it was made as a copy of an earlier work. The decoration is quite interesting and skillfully executed. A monster face with bulging eyes and dynamic curling antlers occupies the lower left of the vessel, while all sorts of spiral forms, thrown helter-skelter, cover the entire surface. This is, of course, the way of early bronzes where we find virtually no area left without decoration. The dominant head at the base and rather awkward, baroque shape of the vessel, which seems to lean heavily to the lower left, most likely derive from the ancient Persian rhyton form, a theme adapted by the Chinese in early bronze. Measuring $5\frac{1}{2}$ inches tall and 5 inches wide, the jade itself is admirably suited to the form, probably retaining much the same shape as the original boulder—a very striking, provocative example!

M. H. de Young Memorial Museum: Avery Brundage Collection.

Plate 45   The art of jade carving flourished during the reign of Ch'ien-lung, because the finished product did not have to comply with rigid standards of religious dogma or established ideas of design. Aesthetic enjoyment was the order of the day.

Precisely this philosophy is embodied here in a cut white jade covered vase which measures $12\frac{1}{2}$ inches tall. The broad, clear surface of the vase is complemented by cranes standing upon a branch which wends its way gracefully across the body, supplying a link for the long, loose-ring chain connecting the dragon-topped cover. The workmanship is exquisite, the polish high, the heavy loose rings suspended from dragon-head handles balancing the composition which is carved from one solid piece of jade material.

American Museum of Natural History: William Boyce Thompson Collection.

Chia-ch'ing (1796–1821) inherited the throne from his illustrious father and proceeded to rule with little regard for anyone but himself. He accused his father's friend and adviser, Ho Shen, of being disloyal and after imprisoning him Chia-ch'ing confiscated his property, thereby acquiring riches described as "a wealth of jade and jewels greater than all the Imperial treasure" [2]. Due to the new monarch's poor judgment and indiscriminate cruelty, a small Buddhist uprising mushroomed to such proportions that it lasted nine years and took countless lives. The decline of the Manchus had begun.

Just as the throne had been willed to a man of fraudulent character, art from here on loses integrity. Fine jades were carved, but the appreciative audience was fast diminishing. The old values disappeared. The throne set a false standard.

Despite the honest efforts of Tao-kuang (1821–50), who had succeeded his father Chia-ch'ing, and the endeavors of subsequent emperors to strengthen the nation once more, the Manchu control was doomed. China had been able to exist, to prosper and grow unto herself, receiving tribute from surrounding countries, trading with neighbors in the East and West, but always retaining her stature as the "foremost nation in the center of the universe." She thought of her emperor as the "great ruler of the world" and, while aware of the existence of other nations, did not believe them worthy of much notice or respect. Her trade agreements with European nations, particularly England, were stringent, often untenable. All foreign factories and trade transactions were restricted to Canton. All aliens engaged in foreign trade were likewise kept in the city of Canton and not permitted access to any other part of the country. Chinese customs officials and specially appointed brokers exacted their tribute and taxes before goods could be brought into the country. Countless agreements were signed and then broken. Undoubtedly many offenses were committed on both sides.

The story of the downfall of the great Manchus in the

19th century tends to be colored by the allegiance of the narrator. While it is true that the emperor cast a haughty, suspicious eye on the foreigner and imposed harsh limitations, it is equally true that the foreign "barbarian" introduced opium which succeeded in undermining a large portion of the population over a period of time. There was, in turn, the danger of too much money flowing out of the country in later years. However, the dire poverty which the people suffered and the complete disunity of the nation was brought about by the overwhelming corruption of the imperial government, culminating in the wicked, immoral behavior of the Empress Dowager (Tzu Hsi) who dominated the royal family from 1861 to the time of her death in 1909. No longer did the sovereign enjoy "the Mandate of Heaven." Hunger, brutality, and crime were the law of the land, while the Manchus isolated themselves in the Forbidden City, luxuriating in the pleasures of plenty.

Just as the character of the government became corrupt, so the art of the 19th century deteriorated. Nevertheless, some of the proficiency and creative energy persisted so that while not quite as satisfying as 18th-century jades, there are examples worthy of our consideration (Plates 46–51).

The great Manchus sowed their own seeds of destruction, and with it went the last vestiges of pure inspiration required for honest artistic endeavor. However, we can look back upon the glory of the Emperor K'ang-hsi who established peace, strength, and moral fiber in the land; who revived and fostered an interest in the arts; whose enthusiasm coupled with tasteful restraint brought about the creation of superb works of art. And we can recall with a measure of indulgence, the irrepressible incorrigible extravagance of Emperor Ch'ien-lung who reveled in the finest artistic accomplishments of the time, encouraging the traditional and stimulating the new.

Plate 46　Mirroring the pomp and sheer resplendence of the late Manchu court is this lavishly cut jadeite incense burner, one of a set of three altar pieces, which measures 7 inches tall, 6 inches wide. Brilliant splashes of emerald green stand out against the sea green ground. A labyrinth of dragons and clouds, cut in high relief, adorns the body and cover of the vessel. Loose rings further enrich the sumptuously bedecked cover; heavier rings are suspended from robust dragon-head handles. The entire composition is a tour de force in technical achievement, enhanced considerably by the intense properties of the stone color. Though quite elaborate, fanciful, impressive, extravagantly executed, the design is preoccupied with appearances …this last, a fundamental weakness of the time.

American Museum of Natural History: William Boyce Thompson Collection.

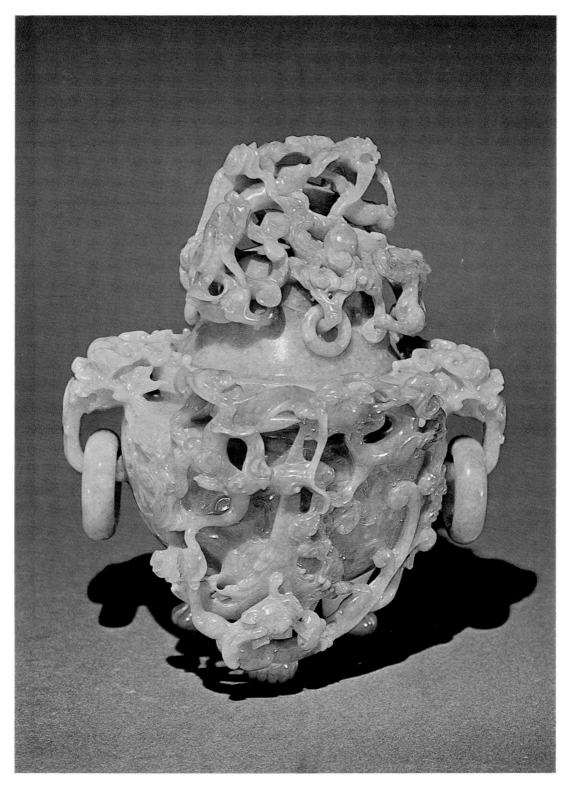

Plate 47   This white jade vase, measuring $8\frac{1}{2}$ inches tall, exhibits remarkable delicacy and grace. Simulated fabric falls easily over the bulk of the vessel and is cinched neatly by a ribbed cord tied into a bowknot. Chrysanthemums with full leafage overlap the arrangement adding a gay, capricious note. The realistic rendering of rope against material, the soft touch of flowers and foliage, the gently swaying tassels, evoke images of springtime, youth, good things to eat, and whatever dreams are to be found in "gift wrapped" jade vases.

Walker Art Center, Minneapolis.

Plate 48
(Two views)   The elaborate, sumptuous Ch'ien-lung style is exemplified in a mottled sage green jade marriage bowl, approximately 20 inches across the larger handles. Decorated with chrysanthemum patterns rendered in a rather crude, inept manner, the bowl lacks the precision and crisp quality of the earlier works. Nevertheless, the four handles capped by full-spread blossoms (which probably held loose rings at one time) and the lively motif on interior and exterior, help this bowl retain a large measure of the gay 18th-century spirit, the chrysanthemum itself a symbol of joviality.

American Museum of Natural History.

Plate 49   What these later pieces lack in character they sometimes make up for in color and charm. A case in point is this jadeite Kuan-yin (Goddess of Mercy) of a beautiful green color. Measuring 26 inches tall (unusually large) the Kuan-yin has her eyes half-closed in deep meditation, her robes drawn together, and flaring out gracefully toward the bottom in gently draped folds. The material is a "glorious gray-green running to a brilliant leaf green in places" [10] and is spotted intermittently with splotches of rust brown. Though the polish is glaring, and the figure rigidly posed, she is imbued with a divine dignity.

University Museum, U. of Pennsylvania: George Byron Gordon Memorial Collection.

Plate 50   Another example where the color overrides form in importance, is the figural group opposite which stands $10\frac{1}{2}$ inches tall. The material alone, a brilliant green jadeite, is sufficient to spark our aesthetic senses. As so often happens in these later examples, however, the subject has lost some of its original purity. Kuan-yin is here depicted as a rather ordinary female, enveloped in thin, cascading streamers with cloud motifs probably intended to impart an ethereal quality. Her face is kind, benevolent, yet unsophisticated. The dragon-head fish at her feet has dash but little real vitality. The two children are stiffly represented and resemble old men in miniature. Something of the majesty and compassion inherent to the deity are gone. In their place we have swirling draperies and color; lots of show, but little substance—an attractive, appealing work, without heart.

Fogg Art Museum, Harvard University: Dane Bequest.

Plate **51** To the color conscious eye perhaps the most appealing material is lavender jade. The jadeite Kuan-yin opposite, measuring $11\frac{1}{4}$ inches tall, displays tones which blend from pale celadon (with a dash of dark green) to light lavender to a mellow violet. The stately head-dress, easy-flowing garments, pretty flowers, and generally graceful aspect of this figure, make it a very charming example, if not a thoroughly satisfying one from an aesthetic viewpoint. For we cannot but notice, once again, that with the advent of bright color, gleaming surfaces, and mechanical facility, the subject has become stereotyped, its initial vitality lost in a maze of fuss and frippery!

American Museum of Natural History: William Boyce Thompson Collection.

⚏ *Conclusion* ⚏

In ancient days, the Chinese used jade implements and symbols to communicate with the heavens. They believed that jade was the embodiment and the conveyor of man's highest thoughts. They likened it to all the virtues, and it was incorporated in Confucian, Taoist, and Buddhist philosophies. In its infinite variety and strength, the Chinese found exaltation and confidence. Their inspiration was born of this trust. And so they set about the task of exposing the intrinsic value of the stone, cutting, shaping, polishing until its beauty and inherent dignity were fully realized. Jade sculpture, then, was their supreme achievement invested with genuine affection, the highest expectations, and unalterable immovable faith!

Glossary

ch'i-lin: a mythological creature known as Kylin, sometimes called the Chinese unicorn

ch'ih lung: archaic dragon form associated with the color yellow

chloromelanite: jadeite which is non-translucent, ranging in color from bright green to black

chromealbite feldspar: official classification name for the mineral called *maw-sit-sit* by the Burmese: it looks very much like chloromelanite, but usually has a bluer cast and is slightly softer and more brittle

fei-t'sui: green-and-white jadeite material, the term adapted from the brilliant plumage of the kingfisher bird

fêng huang: a fabulous bird sometimes called the phoenix

Fo Shou: citron resembling Buddha's hand

fu-i: bat with outspread wings

hu: ancient bronze shape in the form of a jar or vase designed to hold wine

ju-i: meaning "as you wish"

ju-i pao: the wish-granting jewel

ju-i scepter: a scepter awarded to military heroes, great statesmen, artists, ambassadors, etc.

kan-chu lung: dragons pursuing pearls

kuang: ancient bronze shape resembling a covered gravy boat

Kuan-yin: Goddess of Mercy (Buddhist)

kuei: ancient bronze shape in the form of a round deep vessel with two handles, sometimes on a stand

k'uei: archaic form of the dragon, usually depicted in profile

ling chih: herb of immortality

lung: dragon

maw-sit-sit: see chromealbite feldspar

Pa Chi Hsiang: Eight Buddhist Emblems (Symbols) usually consisting of
the wheel, the conch shell, the umbrella, the canopy, the lotus, the
vase, a pair of fish, and the endless knot
Pa Hsien: Eight Immortals, legendary figures who achieved immortality in
various ways
pao yao: a paste made of various abrasives which is used to polish jade
pi: a flat circular jade disc with a hole in the center believed to have been
used by the ancient Chinese in the worship of Heaven
pilgrim vase: a vase with a shape derived from T'ang pottery wares

shou: symbol of long life

t'ao t'ieh: monster mask motif seen on early bronze vessels, originally
thought to have been placed there to deter the hands of the greedy, its
meaning now uncertain
ts'ung: a hollow round jade tube encased in a square body thought to be
the symbol of Earth by the ancient Chinese

yü: usually refers to gem stones, and nephrite in particular
yüan-wo: circular or whorl pattern

Bibliography

The numbers correspond with those in brackets in the text.

1. Ashton, Leigh, and Gray, Basil: *Chinese Art,* London, 1935
2. Backhouse, E., and Bland, J. O. P.: *Annals & Memoirs of the Court of Peking,* London, 1914
3. Bishop, Heber R.: *Investigations and Studies in Jade,* Vols. I and II, New York, 1906
4. Burling, Judith, and Hart, Arthur: *Chinese Art,* New York, 1953
5. Burwell, W. B.: "Exhibition of Chinese Jades-OAC-London," *Oriental Art,* Autumn, 1948
6. Bushell, Stephen W.: *Chinese Art,* Vols. I and II, London, 1914
7. Cheng, Te-k'un: "T'ang and Ming Jades," *Transactions of the Oriental Ceramic Society,* (London), 1953–54
8. Couling: *Encyclopaedia Sinica,* London, 1917
9. du Boulay, Anthony: *Chinese Porcelain,* New York, 1963
10. Fernald, Helen E.: *The Museum Journal,* University of Pennsylvania, March, 1928
11. Giles, Lionel: *The Sayings of Confucius* (reprint from the original published in London, 1907), New York, 1961
12. Giles, Herbert A.: *A Chinese Biographical Dictionary* (reprint of the 1898 edition), New York
13. Goette, John: *Jade Lore,* New York, 1937
14. Gowen, Herbert H.: *An Outline History of China,* Vol. II, Boston, 1913
15. Grousset, Rene: *The Rise and Splendour of the Chinese Empire,* London, 1952
16. Grousset, Rene: *Chinese Art & Culture,* New York, 1959
17. Gump, Richard: *Jade: Stone of Heaven,* New York, 1962
18. Gump, A. Livingston: *Jade Hunt,* New York, 1937
19. Hansford, S. Howard: *Chinese Carved Jades,* London, 1968

20. Hansford, S. Howard: "Chinese Jade," *Transactions of Oriental Ceramic Society*, London, 1948

21. Hansford, S. Howard: *Chinese Jade Carving*, London, 1950

22. Hansford, S. Howard: *A Glossary of Chinese Art and Archaeology*, London, 1961

23. Hardinge, Sir Charles: *Jade—Fact and Fable*, London, 1961

24. Hobson, R. L.: *The Wares of the Ming Dynasty*, London, 1923

25. Hucker, Charles O.: *The Traditional Chinese State in Ming Times*, Tucson, Arizona, 1961

26. Jenyns, Soame: *Chinese Archaic Jades*, British Museum, London, 1951

27. Latourette, Kenneth S.: *The Chinese—Their History and Culture*, New York, 1934

28. Laufer, Berthold: *Jade*, Field Museum of Natural History, Chicago, 1912

29. Lee, Sherman E.: *A History of Far Eastern Art*, Great Britain, 1964

30. Lin, Yutang: *Imperial Peking*, New York, 1961

31. Lion-Goldschmidt & Moreau-Gobard: *Chinese Art*, New York, 1962

32. Macgowan, Rev. J.: *A History of China*, London, 1897

33. Malone, Carroll Brown: "History of the Peking Summer Palaces Under the Ch'ing Dynasty," thesis for the University of Ill., 1928, reprinted from *Illinois Studies in the Social Sciences*, Vol. XIX, nos. 1–2, 1934

34. Mayers, William F.: *The Chinese Reader's Manual*, London, 1874

35. Medley, Margaret: *A Handbook of Chinese Art*, London, 1964

36. Meen, V. B.: "Both Nephrite and Jadeite Occur in Same Area in Japan," *Lapidary Journal*, April, 1966

37. Morgan, Evan: "Times & Manners in the Age of the Emperor K'ang Hsi," *Journal of the North China Branch of the Royal Asiatic Society*, Vol. LXIX, 1938

38. Na, Chi-liang: *Chinese Seals—The Collection of Ralph C. Lee*, Taiwan, Republic of China, 1966

39. Nott, Stanley Charles: *Chinese Jade Carvings of the XVIth to the XIXth Century in Collection of Mrs. Georg Vetlesen*, New York, 1939, Vols. I, II, and III

40. Nott, Stanley Charles: *Voices from the Flowery Kingdom*, New York, 1947

41. Nott, Stanley Charles: *Chinese Jades in the Stanley Charles Nott Collection*, Norton Gallery & School of Art, W. Palm Beach, Florida, 1942

42. Nott, Stanley Charles: *Chinese Jade Throughout the Ages*, reprint of London edition of 1936, Rutland, Vt., 1962

43. Okakura: *The Awakening of Japan*, New York, 1904

44. Pope-Hennessey, Una: *A Jade Miscellany*, London, 1946

45. Pope-Hennessey, Una: *Early Chinese Jades*, New York, 1923

46. Priest, Alan, *Bulletin of the Metropolitan Museum of Art*, Vol. XXXII, no. 12, December, 1937

47. Ricci, Matthew: *China in the Sixteenth Century: The Journals of Matthew Ricci: 1583–1610*, translated by S. J. Gallagher, New York, 1953

48. Salmony, Alfred: (a catalogue of jade) Vassar College Art Gallery, New York, 1941

49. Seeger, Elizabeth: *The Pageant of Chinese History,* London and New York, 1934

50. Soothill, W. E.: *A History of China,* New York, 1951

51. Swann, Peter C.: *Art of China, Korea and Japan,* New York, 1963

52. Tamiya, Paul H.: "New Discoveries of Jade Made in Japan," *Lapidary Journal,* January, 1966

53. Watson, W.: *Chinese Jades in the Chester Beatty Library,* Dublin, 1963

54. Werner, E. T. C.: *Myths & Legends of China,* London, 1922

55. Willetts, W.: *Chinese Art,* Vols. I and II, Harmondsworth, Middlesex, 1958

56. Williams, C. A. S.: *Encyclopedia of Chinese Symbolism and Art Motives,* New York, 1960

57. Winterbotham, W.: *An Historical, Geographical, and Philosophical View of the Chinese Empire,* London, 1795

Index

Afghanistan, 102

Alaska, 20

American Museum of Natural History (Thompson Collection), 60, 124, 144, 148, 152, 158

amphibole, 21

Amur River, 74

Annam, 102

artemisia leaf, 100

Ashton and Grey, 120

Attiret, 103

Aztecs, 20

Azure Dragon, 39

Backhouse and Bland, 68, 105

bat, 62, 94, 112

Bishop Collection; *see* Metropolitan Museum of Art

Black Warrior, 39

bromoform, 24

bronze-form styles, 48, 76, 84, 86, 88, 92, 100, 118, 120, 124, 132, 134, 138, 140, 142

Brundage Collection; *see* de Young Memorial Museum

buffalo, 56, 82

Buddha's hand citron (Fo Shou), 52

Buddhism, 41, 42, 43, 46, 68, 73, 80, 98, 161

Burling, Judith and Arthur, 68

Burma, 19, 24, 102, 104

Burwell, W. B., 107

Bushell, S. W., 103

calcified ("chicken bone") jade, 58

California, 20

Canada, 20

Canton, 20

carborundum, 27

carp, 80

Central America, 20

Cheng-te, Emperor, 42

Cheng, Dr. Te-k'un, 30

Chester Beatty Library, 104

Chia-ch'ing, Emperor (Ch'ing dynasty), 34, 106, 146

Chia-ch'ing, Emperor (Ming dynasty), 42

chiao-yeh, 132

"chicken bone" jade; *see* calcified ("chicken bone") jade

Ch'ien-lung period, 102–107; jade pieces, 58, 108, 110, 112, 114, 116, 118, 120, 122, 124, 126, 128, 130, 132, 134, 136, 138, 140, 142, 144

ch'i-lin (Kylin), 84

ch'ih lung, 100

chimera, 122
Ch'ing dynasty, 32, 65
Ching-t'ai, Emperor, 42
chloromelanite, 24, 25
Chou dynasty, 31
chromealbite feldspar, 25
chromium, 21
chrysanthemum, 150, 152
chrysophrase, 23
Ch'ung-chen, Emperor, 45
Cleveland Museum of Art (Sever-
    ance Collection), 136
Confucianism, 41, 42, 43, 44, 161
Confucius, 50
Crowningshield, Robert, 22, 23
cycle of sixty, 107

Dane Bequest; see Fogg Art Mu-
    seum
de Young Memorial Museum
    (Brundage Collection), 52, 86,
    90, 122, 130, 132, 142
Dowager, Empress; see Tzu Hsi
dragon (k'uei), 54, 60, 76, 78, 80,
    84, 86, 88, 92, 100, 114, 116,
    120, 126, 130, 134, 136, 138,
    140, 144, 148, 156

Eastern Turkestan, 19, 65, 102
Eight Buddhist Emblems, 62
Eight Immortals (Pa Hsien), 114
elephant, 116
Eskimos, 20

fei t'sui, 20
fêng-huang, 66, 94, 114; see also
    Phoenix
Fogg Art Museum (Dane Bequest),
    76, 78, 96, 156
"Forbidden City," 39
Fo Shou; see Buddha's hand citron
four supernatural creatures, 39
Fuller Memorial Collection; see
    Seattle Art Museum

garnet, green, 23; pink, 22
Gemological Institute of America,
    22, 24

Giles, Herbert, A., 70
Goddess of Mercy, 154; see also
    Kuan-yin
Goes, Benedict, 104
Gordon Collection; see University
    Museum, U. of Penn.
gourd, 96, 112
Grousset, Rene, 39
Gump, Richard, 27, 33
Hanlin Academy, 38
Hansford, S. Howard, 22, 26, 54,
    62, 73, 92
Hardinge, Sir Charles, 24
Hennessy, Una Pope-; see Pope-
    Hennessy, Una
herb of immortality, 72
Hinayana Buddhism, 42
Hobson, R. L., 42
Honshu island (Japan), 19
Hsuan-t'ung, Emperor, 128
Hucker, Chas. O., 38, 39, 40, 41,
    44
Hung Wu, Emperor, 37–39

"Imperial" jade, 25
iron, 24

jade, carving, 22, 26, 27, 28, 31,
    41; dating of carvings, 30, 35;
    imitations, 23, 24; location of
    rough, 19, 20, 21; mineral
    properties, 21–23; uses, 23,
    40, 72, 73, 106; varieties; see
    chloromelanite, jadeite, Japa-
    nese jade, nephrite
jadeite, 19, 20, 21, 22, 23, 24,
    33, 104
Japanese jade, 19, 25
Jehol, 74
Jesuits, 70, 74, 98
Jomon (Japanese), 20
ju-i motif, 72, 118, 130, 138
ju-i pao, 73
ju-i scepter, 72, 94, 118

K'ang-hsi, Emperor, 26, 31, 32,
    68, 69–75; jade pieces, 78, 80,
    82, 84, 86, 88, 90, 92, 94, 96

key-pattern banding, 84, 88, 90, 118, 120, 130, 132, 134, 138
Korea, 65, 102
Khotan, 19
Kotaki, 19
Kuan-yin, 154, 156, 158; *see also* Goddess of Mercy
k'uei; see dragon
k...i (bronze form), 134
Kylin; *see ch'i-lin*

Lake Baikal, 19
Latourette, K. S., 102
Laufer, Berthold, 84, 106, 132
Lee, Sherman E., 71
ling-chih, 72, 118
lotus, 28, 46, 73, 128
Luh Tzu-kang, 30
Lung-men, 42

Macao, 98
Macgowan, Rev. J., 38
Mahayana Buddhism, 41
Malaysia, 71
Manchuria, 65
Manchus, 45, 65, 147
Mandate of Heaven, 40, 71, 73, 98
Maori, 20
maw-sit-sit, 25
Mayans, 20
melon, 58
Mencius, 89
Meng, Dr. Chih, 42, 43
Metropolitan Museum of Art (Bishop Collection), 80, 82, 84, 92, 94, 100, 108, 118, 126
Ming dynasty, 26, 30, 32, 37–45; jade pieces, 28, 46–54
Minneapolis Institute of Arts (Searle Collection), 28, 110, 112, 128
Mogaung, 19
Mohs' scale, 22
Mongolia, 65, 102
Mongols, 37, 38

Na Chih-liang, 30

Nanking, 38
Nepal, 102
nephrite, 19, 20, 21, 22, 23, 24, 33
Newark Museum, 88, 118
new jade (onion jade), 23
New Zealand, 20
nineteenth-century jade examples, 148, 150, 152, 154, 156, 158
Norton Gallery of Art (Nott Collection), 50, 56, 66, 100
Nott, Stanley Chas., 33, 50, 54, 56, 140; Collection; *see* Norton Gallery of Art
Nurhachi, 45

Oderick, Friar, 103
Okakura, K., 54
Omi, 19
onion jade; *see* new jade
"Orchid Pavilion," 108
owl, 48

Pa Chi Hsiang, 62
Pa Hsien; *see* Eight Immortals
palm, 116
pao yao, 27
Peking, 39, 72
peony, 62, 94, 110, 130
Phoenix, 39, 66, 76, 94, 114; *see also* Vermilion Bird
pi, 60
pine, 90
"pink" jade, 22
Pope-Hennessy, Una, 37, 90, 104
precious pearl, 76, 86, 88, 92, 96, 126
Priest, Alan, 126
pyroxene, 21

quartz, chalcedony, 22; green, 23; rose, 22

refractometer, 24
Republic of China, 71
Ricci, Matteo, 43
ritual services, 40, 73
Russian Turkestan, 102

Sacred Edict, 70
Salmony, A., 34
Searle Collection; *see* Minneapolis Institute of Arts
Seattle Art Museum (Fuller Memorial Collection), 28, 48, 114
serpentine, 23
Severance Collection; *see* Cleveland Museum of Art
Shang dynasty, 60
Shangraw, Clarence, 142
shou, 96, 116, 120
Shun-chih, Emperor, 66; jade piece, 66
Siberia, 19
silkworm emblems, 118
Singapore, 71
Smithsonian Institution (Vetlesen Collection), 54, 62, 134, 138, 140
smithsonite, 23
soapstone, 23
Soothill, W. E., 102
spectroscope, 24
summer palaces, 74, 105, 116, 126
Swann, Peter C., 45
swastika, 94

Taiwan, 20
Tao-kuang, Emperor, 34, 146
Taoism, 41, 42, 43, 46, 68, 72, 90, 108, 161
t'ao t'ieh, 76, 86, 88, 110, 118
tea, 102
ten celestial stems, 107
Thompson Collection; *see* American Museum of Natural Art

thulite, 22
thunder-cloud motifs, 84
Tibet, 65, 102
tiger, 100
Tun-huang, 42
twelve terrestrial branches, 107
Tzu Hsi (Empress Dowager), 147

unicorn, 84
University Museum, U. of Penn. (Gordon Collection), 154
Uru River, 19

Van Braam, 103
Verbiest, Father, 70
Vermilion Bird (Phoenix), 39
Vetlesen Collection; *see* Smithsonian Institution

Walker Art Center, 46, 58, 120, 150
Wang Hao-chen, 30
Wang Shin-lu, 30
Wan-li, Emperor, 43
Werner, E. T. C., 73
White Tiger, 39
Willetts, Wm., 138
Williams, C. A. S., 39, 66, 92
Winterbotham, W., 70
Wyoming, 20

Yannopoulos, Admiral, 21
Yarkand, 19, 104
yü, 20
yüan wo, 88, 118
Yung-cheng, Emperor, 33, 98; jade pieces, 100
Yung-lo, Emperor, 39